W9-BGY-414

TREAD LIGHTLY

DISCARD

PROPERTY OF:
RANCHO MIRAGE PUBLIC LIBRARY
71-100 HIGHWAY 111
RANCHO MIRAGE, CA 92270
(760) 341-READ 7323

TREAD LIGHTLY
VENOMOUS AND POISONOUS ANIMALS OF THE SOUTHWEST

Rich and Margie Wagner

RIO NUEVO PUBLISHERS

TUCSON, ARIZONA

Rio Nuevo Publishers®
P.O. Box 5250, Tucson, Arizona 85703-0250
(520) 623-9558, www.rionuevo.com

Text and photographs © 2005 by Rich and Margie Wagner. All rights reserved. No part of this book may be reproduced, stored, introduced into a retrieval system, or otherwise copied in any form without the prior written permission of the publisher, except for brief quotations in reviews or citations.

Library of Congress Cataloging-in-Publication Data

Wagner, Rich, 1958-
Tread lightly : venomous and poisonous animals of the southwest / Rich and Margie Wagner.
      p. cm.
Includes bibliographical references and index.
ISBN-13: 978-1-887896-76-4 (pbk.)
ISBN-10: 1-887896-76-7 (pbk.)
1. Poisonous animals—Southwestern States. I. Wagner, Margie, 1968- II. Title.
QL157.S69W34 2006
591.6'5'0979—dc22
                     2005023325

Design: Karen Schober, Seattle, Washington

On the front cover (clockwise from top right): black-tailed rattlesnake, female black widow, western diamondback rattlesnake, tiger rattlesnake, Mojave rattlesnakes, Gila monster. On the back cover (left to right): extracting venom from a western diamondback rattlesnake, bark scorpion with babies, red spotted toad, tarantula.

Pictured on p. 1: brown spider; p. 2: black widow with egg sac; p. 3: black-tailed rattlesnake; p. 5: banded rock rattlesnake, desert millipede, western banded gecko.

Printed in Korea.

10   9   8   7   6   5   4   3   2   1

TABLE of CONTENTS

Introduction

The southwestern United States has a fascinating diversity of vegetation and wildlife, much of which has evolved to survive under very hostile environmental conditions. For anyone arriving in the Southwest for the first time from a more temperate climate, the landscape appears completely alien. Dense forests of green are replaced by cacti, mesquite trees, and creosote bushes. Common trees seem nowhere to be found, and even familiar species like oaks have small, unfamiliar leaves. Within this alien landscape lurk the often dreaded and dangerous venomous and poisonous animals of the Southwest.

Just exactly where are these animals to be found? How dangerous are they? How likely are you to encounter them? What should you do if you or someone else has a "bad encounter"? Is *everything* in the Southwest venomous or poisonous? How can you know what is and what's not?

As professional photographers living in the Southwest and as medical professionals, we want to take the fear out of visiting or living in the wilderness of the Southwest.

Encounters with venomous or poisonous animals should be cherished and enjoyed—safely—be it in your home, back yard, or when out hiking or camping. These animals are an integral part of the ecosystem, and developing an understanding of how they survive can be immensely rewarding. An awareness of how an animal is *likely* to behave can take the fear out of an encounter—and help to keep you safe. Knowing what to do—and what not to do—if you are bitten or stung (envenomated) can save your life. Most importantly, learning about venomous and poisonous animals can be just plain fun!

IT'S ALL ABOUT SURVIVAL

Life in the Southwest revolves around water. Humans settle close to it, or find ways to pipe it in. Plants and animals have evolved ways to conserve it. Many desert plants have waxy leaves, which minimize the amount of water lost by evaporation. Often, these plants have developed chemical or mechanical defenses like toxins and thorns to

LEFT: Gila monster. ABOVE: Brown spider.

A researcher extracts venom from a Western diamondback (*Crotalus atrox*). **8**

prevent their precious water stores from being eaten by animals anxious to maintain their own hydration. In a similar manner, many of the animals of the Southwest have developed extraordinary defenses to help ensure their survival.

The big, lumbering Gila monster might make a fine meal for many, if not for its quick reflexes and venomous bite. The lightning-fast strike of a rattlesnake leaves its prey mortally wounded—it will drop dead from cardio-vascular collapse a short distance away from where it was bitten, and pheromones within the venom will allow the snake to carefully track it down, thus avoiding potential injury in a struggle. Many kingsnakes have evolved to look like their venomous cousins, the coral snakes, in a move that fools many predators into leaving them alone, and in an incredible evolutionary twist, kingsnakes are immune to rattlesnake venom and actually eat rat-tlesnakes! Clearly, animal defenses are essential to the sur-vival of many animals in the Southwest.

VENOM AND POISON: SOME IMPORTANT DISTINCTIONS

Defining what is "venomous" or "poisonous" can be difficult, simply because human beings are often not the intended "victims" of an animal's poison or toxin. For example, although all spiders produce venom that allows them to immobilize or kill their prey, many of these spiders are so small that it is physically impossible for them to bite and envenomate a person. In general, a venom or poison is a substance that can interfere with the normal biochemistry of a victim. These substances are either a means of defense or a means to kill or subdue prey. Some venoms, encountered in the usual amounts, have a minimal effect on humans, and aren't considered dangerous. Others, like the venom from the bark scorpion, can cause us to endure tremendous pain and other neurologic symptoms, and we therefore consider these animals to be both venomous and dangerous.

When used in small amounts, poisons and venoms often become useful medicines. Familiar poisonous plants such as deadly nightshade, foxglove, and jimson weed are good examples. The so-called poisons in these plants are toxic only in relatively high doses. When active substances are purified and doses are standardized, they become useful medications. Today, more than half of all pharmaceuticals were initially derived from natural sources. Scientific work on the potential beneficial effects of venoms and poisons is relatively new, as most research to date has focused on how to stop the often disastrous effects these substances cause when delivered in large doses via stingers or fangs.

More than a dozen useful diagnostic tests and treat-ments are now derived from snake venoms. A new treat-ment for diabetes has even been developed from Gila monster venom.

VENOMOUS ANIMALS By definition, venomous animals produce toxins in specialized secretory cells in a venom gland. The collective mix of different toxins produced by an animal is known as *venom,* which is produced and stored by an animal until it is needed. During a bite or sting, venom is *actively* delivered by injection through what is called a "venom apparatus." The apparatus consists of the venom-producing cells, a means for storage of the venom, and a means for injecting the venom, such as a grooved or hollow tooth (a fang) or a stinging apparatus.

Venoms contain many different toxins that consist mostly of peptides and proteins. These toxins are usually effective only when introduced into prey or a victim *parenterally*—for example, by injection into skin, muscle, the circulatory system, or other tissues. Ingesting, or swallowing, venom or a venomous animal usually results in inactivation of the venom by the gut. This so-called *enteral* exposure to venoms does not usually result in toxic exposure.

Venoms are primarily used by an animal as a defense against predators, to help immobilize or kill prey, or to help digest prey.

POISONOUS ANIMALS Poisonous animals lack a venom apparatus to actively deliver toxins as a defense mechanism. Instead, the survival of these species depends on the *passive* delivery of toxins. Ingesting a poisonous animal results in

A venomous lizard, the Gila monster (*Heloderma suspectum*).

The poisonous Sonoran desert toad (*Bufo alvarius*).

toxicity; also, poisonous secretions from animals such as toads or frogs may be absorbed through the skin, resulting in toxicity.

The toxins in poisonous animals may be produced by the animal, or they may be acquired by accumulation from the environment, primarily through the food chain. These toxins are often secondary metabolites of ingested compounds. Poisonous animals obviously must have resistance to the toxins to ensure their own survival. They also must be able to ingest the substances (usually found in plants) that they use as precursors to produce their toxins, otherwise they may lose their toxicity.

The harmless regal horned lizard (*Phrynosoma solare*).

NON-VENOMOUS, NON-POISONOUS ANIMALS Many animals in the Southwest have the misfortune of being misidentified as venomous or poisonous. These animals are often killed, based on the unfounded fear that they might be harmful. Many of them look scary or dangerous, but most are harmless or nearly so. To help you distinguish among dangerous and non-dangerous species, we have included several examples of non-venomous and non-poisonous animals in each section of this book.

Ouch!

ENVENOMATION is the injection of venom via a bite or sting.

VENOMOUS BITE refers to injection of venom by structures of the mouth, including fangs or teeth.

STING refers to venom injected by means of a tapered structure (stinger) at the posterior or back end of the animal.

What To Do If You Have Been Bitten, Stung, or Poisoned

IF SOMEONE IS UNCONSCIOUS OR SERIOUSLY INJURED OR SICK, CALL 911 IMMEDIATELY!

We have attempted to give current recommendations for the appropriate first aid treatment of bites, stings, and poisonings. Fortunately, the art and science of medicine are constantly evolving, and recommendations invariably change with time. To provide medical practitioners with information that may help with treatment, try to observe the animal's appearance as closely, but safely, as you can. An individual's response to a bite or sting may also be very different from what typically occurs. Therefore, if you have any questions or concerns about a bite, sting, or potential poisoning, we strongly encourage you to contact your personal physician, go to your local emergency department, **call 911, or call the national Poison Center Hotline at 800-222-1222 immediately.** Your life, or someone else's, may depend on your call!

The Arizona Poison and Drug Information Center in Tucson is a worldwide referral center for venomous snakebite and for other venomous bites and stings. This poison center can be contacted at 520-626-7899 (or from *within* southern Arizona using the national hotline number, 800-222-1222). The other regional poison centers listed here are also capable of advising on the management of bites, stings, and poisonings.

ARIZONA Arizona Poison and Drug Information Center (Tucson), 520-626-7899, www.pharmacy.arizona.edu/outreach/poison/
Banner Poison Control Center (Phoenix), 602-495-4884 www.bannerpoisoncontrol.com/

CALIFORNIA California Poison Control System (San Diego Division), 858-715-6300, www.calpoison.org

COLORADO (*also serves Idaho, Montana, and Nevada*) Rocky Mountain Poison and Drug Center (Denver), 303-739-1100, www.rmpdc.org

NEW MEXICO New Mexico Poison and Drug Information Center (Albuquerque), 505-272-4261, http://hsc.unm.edu/pharmacy/poison

TEXAS Central Texas Poison Center (Temple), 254-724-7405, www.poisoncontrol.org
North Texas Poison Center (Dallas), 214-589-0911, www.poisoncontrol.org
Southeast Texas Poison Center (Galveston), 409-766-4403, www.utmb.edu/setpc
South Texas Poison Center (San Antonio), 210-567-5762, www.uthscsa.edu/surgery/poisoncenter
Texas Panhandle Poison Center (Amarillo), 806-354-1630, www.poisoncontrol.org
West Texas Poison Center (El Paso, 24-hour, bilingual), 800-222-1222, www.poisoncontrol.org

UTAH Utah Poison Control Center (Salt Lake City), 801-587-0600, http://uuhsc.utah.edu/poison

Arthropods

Arthropods are the most diverse group of animals on earth and comprise more than 85 percent of all living animal species. This fascinating group of animals features external skeletons (or *exoskeletons*), segmented bodies, and jointed legs. Familiar members of this enormously large phylum include spiders, centipedes, scorpions, crabs, and all of the insects.

The phylum of arthropods is subdivided further based on body segmentation and the number and attachment of the legs. The arachnids—best known for spiders and scorpions—all have two body segments (a cephalothorax and an abdomen) and four pairs of segmented legs. The many-legged chilopods, or centipedes, have long bodies with numerous segments and one pair of legs per segment. The diplopods, or millipedes, are similar to centipedes but have two pairs of legs per segment. Insects have three distinct body segments—a head, thorax, and abdomen, and three pairs of legs. They also often have two pairs of wings that arise from the thorax.

ARACHNIDS

The arachnids are a class of arthropods that includes many well-known invertebrates, including spiders, daddy longlegs, scorpions, pseudoscorpions, windscorpions, whip scorpions, mites, ticks, and others. In all, there are currently eleven "orders" of arachnids, with more than 60,000 known species and probably many more as yet undiscovered and unnamed. Arachnids are usually both predatory and solitary, although contrary to popular opinion, most are not dangerous.

All arachnid bodies are divided into two parts: the *cephalothorax* and the abdomen. The cephalothorax contains simple (not complex) eyes, mouth parts, sensory organs, and paired limbs. The first pair of limbs, called *chelicerae,* may form pincers or fangs. The second pair, called *pedipalps,* may serve as pincers, sensory appendages, or legs. The rest of the cephalothorax usually has four pairs of walking legs. The abdomen contains the genital opening and *book lungs,* or modified gills, used for gas exchange and oxygenation.

LEFT: Tarantula (*Amphonopelma chalcodes*).

For example, scorpions are arachnids that are quickly recognized by their segmented, curved, stinging tails and their large pedipalps, or pincer-like extremities. The body of a scorpion is composed of a short, compact cephalothorax and an elongated, segmented abdomen called the *mesosoma.* The feeding appendages (or chelicerae), pedipalps, and segmented legs all attach to the cephalothorax. The pedipalps have claw-like *chelae* for grasping, and they have both the sensitivity of antennae and the strength needed to hold and subdue prey. The underside of the mesosoma contains the genital openings, as well as slits called spiracles that open into the tracheal system and allow the scorpion to breathe, and *pectines,* a pair of feather-like appendages that when lightly dragged along the ground may act as pheromone and vibration detectors. The last six segments of the abdomen are modified into a tail-like structure called a *metasoma* that terminates in the *telson,* or stinger. When alarmed or threatened, a scorpion will curl its tail up and over the body into a position where it can sting anything within reach of the pedipalps (they will often grab prey or an aggressor with their pedipalps and then sting repeatedly with rapid flicks of the tail).

All scorpions fluoresce a yellow-green color under ultraviolet light (or black light), with the exception of newly molted and baby scorpions. This fluorescence allows them to be easily located at night from several feet away by shining a black light in their general direction. The fluorescence is caused by an as-yet unidentified substance located in a very thin layer of the scorpion's cuticle, or exoskeleton.

After molting, the fluorescence increases as the cuticle hardens, indicating that the substance that fluoresces is either secreted by the scorpion shortly after molting or is produced as the cuticle hardens, possibly as a by-product of the hardening process. The substance that fluoresces is very stable, and even scorpion fossils that are hundreds of millions of years old still fluoresce.

There are seven families and 25 genera of scorpions found in North America, although in the United States only the bark scorpion delivers envenomating stings of medical significance. It should be noted that *bites* from scorpions are painless. The *sting* is another story!

Of chelicerae, pedipalps, and chelae *Chelicerae* are modified appendages close to the mouth parts of arachnids that are used as jaws or fangs. *Pedipalps* are appendages that attach between the chelicerae and the first pair of walking legs. With spiders, the pedipalps of females are small and leg-like, but in males they are modified into copulatory organs with bulbous ends that are used to transfer sperm. In scorpions, the pedipalps of both males and females look like arms with crab-like pincers that are used for grasping. The "claws" on the end of the pedipalps are called *chelae*, not to be confused with the scorpion's little chelicerae near the mouth parts. Windscorpions or sun spiders have antennae-like pedipalps with sensitive adhesive organs on the ends; their chelicerae are large, powerful biting appendages. While the bite from the tiny chelicerae of scorpions is painless, if you're bitten by the massive chelicerae of a wind-scorpion or a tarantula, you're going to know it!

Tarantula (*Aphonopelma* and *Dugesiella* species)
VENOMOUS

Range and habitat Arizona alone has at least 30 different species, and Texas has 14; tarantulas are also found in southern Utah, New Mexico, southern California, and south into Mexico. The most common species in the Sonoran Desert of southern Arizona and southeastern California is *Aphonopelma chalcodes,* known as the Arizona blond tarantula, desert tarantula, or Chilean tarantula. It is commonly found in desert areas, particularly saguaro–palo verde habitat, and is often seen at dusk or sunrise near openings of burrows or in rocky areas or washes.

Diet Tarantulas eat crickets, beetles, other arthropods, small lizards, and rodents; species in South America may take prey as large as birds.

Life span Males: 10–12 years (often die within months of mating); females: 20–30 years.

Physical characteristics Tarantulas range in size from 2 to 4 inches (5–10 cm) and can weigh up to an ounce (30 grams). The roughly 30 species of tarantula in the Southwest are grouped into one of two genera (*Aphonopelma* and

Dugesiella). All tarantulas in the Southwest are light to dark brown. The females are usually a uniform color, while the males are often brown with black legs. The abdomen and legs are densely covered with hairs. Although tarantulas have eight closely grouped eyes, they do not have very good vision. Males can be distinguished from females by their smaller comparative size and by the presence of a small hook or "spur" behind the knees of the first pair of legs. Both males and females have well-developed fangs that, unlike those of most other spiders, lie *parallel* to the main

axis of the body and open up and down. The fangs may be up to ⅜ inch (1 cm) in length and are connected to a venom apparatus.

Behavior Tarantulas frequently hide in silk-lined burrows in the ground that they loosely plug up for the day after a night of foraging. During the evening, tarantulas tend to patrol areas near their burrows in search of prey. They are inactive during the winter months and live off their stored fat reserves. Tarantulas molt roughly once a year and often appear dead while molting, as they flip upside down and lie flat on their backs until they escape from their old exoskeleton.

These spiders are very sensitive to vibration. When they sense insects near the opening of their burrow, they practically explode out of the entrance and pounce on their prey. Gently tapping a twig on the ground just outside of a burrow can imitate the vibrations produced by prey and can often entice a tarantula to spring out of its burrow in search of a meal.

Tarantulas are generally docile towards humans and will seldom bite unless provoked. If threatened, they will rear up on their hind legs and raise their front pair of legs in a threat posture, ready to strike. At other times, they may use their hind legs to brush off barbed *urticating* hairs from the top of their abdomen. These hairs can be very irritating to the eyes of an aggressor; hairs from some tropical species are capable of disabling or killing mice. Older tarantulas often have patches of hairs missing from their abdomen as a result of this behavior.

Reproduction Tarantulas take at least ten years to reach sexual maturity. At this point, males disperse in search of suitable females and are often observed crossing the roads during the months of June through October. When a male locates the burrow of a potential mate, he performs a courtship dance at the entrance of the burrow, tapping out signals as vibrations with his feet. If the female is interested, she emerges and an encounter begins. The male uses the spurs on his forelegs to suspend the female above him, and then uses one of his two pedipalps, which look like modified legs, to transfer sperm to the *epigynum*, a plate covering the genital opening on the underside of the female. After mating, the male retreats quickly to avoid being eaten by the female, and the female deposits eggs in her burrow. The roughly 200–300 eggs hatch after six to eight weeks, and the young spiderlings remain in the burrow with the female for days to weeks. The young tarantulas then disperse and go out on their own, building their own small burrows.

Effects of venom The tarantula's fangs are used to inject venom into its prey to paralyze it and begin digesting it from the inside out. For humans, the bite of the desert tarantula has been compared to the sting from a bee or hornet. Although painful, it is usually not particularly dangerous, unless you are unfortunate enough to have an allergic reaction to the venom.

The urticating hairs of tarantulas of the Southwest are not venomous. The most significant complications from the hairs occur when they get in someone's eyes, as they can cause prolonged inflammation and infection.

FIRST AID AND MEDICAL TREATMENT Wounds from tarantula bites should be thoroughly cleaned, and the bite victim's tetanus immunization status should be verified as current (within five years). Most bites do not require medical treatment other than first aid. Ibuprofen or acetaminophen can be taken for pain. Ice may also help to minimize pain and swelling. Any eye involvement with the urticating hairs from a tarantula should be evaluated by an ophthalmologist.

Black widow (*Latrodectus* species)
VENOMOUS

Range and habitat *Latrodectus hesperus,* the western black widow, is common throughout western U.S. and deserts of North America; the "true" black widow, *Latrodectus mactans,* is found in the eastern U.S. from Massachusetts and New Hampshire to Florida, and westward into Texas,

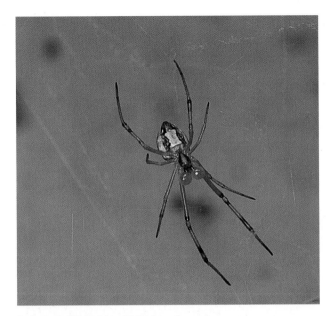

A tiny male black widow (*Latrodactus hesperus*).

Physical characteristics Male and female widows differ in both size and coloration. Adult females are twice as large as males, with a body size of approximately ¼–¾ inch (6–19 mm) in length and a leg span of about 1 ½ inches (4 cm). The body and legs are black or very dark brown, and the abdomen is rounded or oval, with a bright orange-red hourglass marking on the underside. Immature females have red, brown, and tan markings on the upper surface of their abdominal segments, and the hourglass on the underside is tan instead of red. The diminutive males (¼ inch or 6 mm) are lighter in color and have four red and white stripes on each side, and a tan or white hourglass. The males may also have orange coloring in the joints of each leg.

Oklahoma, Kansas, and California (although not in Arizona). Widow spiders favor undisturbed, recessed areas, including low brush, abandoned burrows, fencerows, woodpiles, unfinished cinderblock, garages, outhouses, and within lawn or patio furniture; a strong, irregular-shaped web can indicate black widow habitation.

Diet These spiders eat prey that becomes snared in their webs, including a wide variety of insects and other arthropods; widows have been observed eating prey items as large as a 4-inch (10 cm) desert centipede.

Life span 1–3 years.

Behavior Black widows are largely sedentary spiders that will maintain the same small territory if not disturbed. They are primarily nocturnal and hide during the day. At night, they may be found on their large, strong webs located close to the ground—often hanging upside-down. There is usually a funnel-shaped web that connects to the widow's hiding place. Ideal microhabitats will be in nearly constant use. If a widow is removed from such a location, another widow will quickly take its place.

Black widow males are very small, and their bites are not medically significant. Female black widows are moderately aggressive and usually bite in self-defense, when escape seems unlikely. Bites often occur when the victim unknowingly reaches into a widow's habitat or leans against the spider in an outdoor structure like a hot tub or spa or storage shed. When using primitive outdoor facilities such as outhouses, it is wise to lift the seat and check for spiders before sitting down.

Reproduction Female black widows mate only once in their lifetimes, during the summer. A male will approach a female and send vibratory messages through her web. If receptive, the female will allow the male to approach and remain still long enough for the male to use one of his pedipalps to transfer sperm to her epigynum on the underside of her abdomen. She will store the sperm for future egg-laying, and she may consume the male after mating is completed.

The female will then lay 150–300 eggs and encase them in a light tan or cream-colored egg sac that she spins with silk. The female may produce several egg sacs in her lifetime, but only one is produced at a time. The eggs will hatch after about 30 days, and tiny spiderlings will emerge. The spiderlings climb as high as they can on whatever material is available, then let out a strand of silk into the wind as a "balloon" to carry them away. Spiderlings can travel miles from their birthplace by ballooning. It will then take seven molts to reach full size.

Effects of venom At least 2,500 people a year are bitten by black widows in the United States, but deaths from widow spider envenomation are rare. Unfortunately, the bites can be extremely painful, and serious reactions may occur.

Black widow venom contains a neurotoxin called alpha-latrotoxin that binds to proteins in nerve cells and makes them continuously release neurotransmitters. The constant release of neurotransmitters causes muscles to contract uncontrollably. This alone can be very painful. The alpha-latrotoxin also causes pain nerves to fire uncontrollably, sending pain signals to the brain. The toxin can eventually cause a depletion of neurotransmitters, resulting in weakness and spasms that may persist for weeks to months.

A large female black widow (*Latrodactus hesperus*).

The bite from the black widow may initially cause little pain or discomfort, other than a local reaction. The venom glands are under voluntary control of the spider, thus the amount of venom injected is highly variable. As the venom spreads, over a period of 10–60 minutes, the pain intensifies, and muscle cramping and rigidity may occur in the arms, chest, back, shoulders, or abdomen. Nausea, vomiting, headache, high blood pressure, and anxiety are not uncommon. Severe envenomations can cause shock, coma, and respiratory failure due to muscle paralysis.

FIRST AID AND MEDICAL TREATMENT As with all bites and stings, clean the area of the bite immediately with soap and water to help prevent infection. A cool compress can be used over the bite site, and over-the-counter pain medications may be taken. Children less than five years of age or anyone with severe symptoms should seek prompt medical attention.

Brown (or Violin or Recluse) Spiders

(*Loxosceles* species)
VENOMOUS

Range and habitat About 12 species of brown spider are found in the Southwest deserts (they are commonly called "brown recluse," although that name most properly refers to *Loxosceles reclusa,* the brown spider found throughout southeastern U.S.). The most common Southwest species include:

Arizona recluse, *L. arizonica* (central and southern Arizona, southeastern California); desert recluse, *L. deserta* (south-central to southern California, east to south-central Arizona, and north to southern Nevada, and the Saint George, Utah, area); and Tucson recluse, *L. sabina* (found in Tucson area of southern Arizona). They are often found under rocks, scraps of wood, or dead cactus; in woodrat nests or other animal burrows; and in human dwellings. They prefer dark, dry locations with numerous places to hide.

Diet Like most spiders, they feed on other arthropods.

Life span 1–2 years.

Physical characteristics Brown spiders are light tan to straw to brown in color and have six eyes (not the usual eight) arranged in a horseshoe pattern, with three clusters of two eyes each. They can be easily identified by the characteristic dark violin or fiddle shape on the cephalothorax, where the "neck" of the fiddle points towards the abdomen. The only similar spider with a violin-like marking is the house spider, *Filistata hibernalis,* and it has eight eyes. The body of the adult recluse is about ⅜ inch long (1 cm), and the leg span is about 1 inch (25 mm).

Behavior Brown spiders are nocturnal and generally secretive in their habits. They are seldom seen during the daytime. Generally non-aggressive, they usually bite only when pressed into contact with skin, as with clothing or bedding or bath towels. Their web is often large and irregular.

Reproduction Brown spiders typically mate once during their lifetime. After mating during the warm summer months, the females build egg sacs and deposit about 50 eggs in each sac. The spiderlings emerge from the egg sac about 27 days later. Spiderlings will molt from five to eight times before they become adults. The first molt takes place inside the egg sac.

Effects of venom The bite from brown spiders is often initially painless, and the reaction that follows may range from none or minimal to severe. Most victims do experience pain after three to four hours, and they may have excruciating pain after six to eight hours due to localized ischemia, or low blood flow, in the area around the bite. The pale white ischemic area arises from vasoconstrictors in the venom. A bleb, or blister, then forms in the center of the bite site, surrounded by a reddish ring, giving the appearance of a bull's eye. The bleb in the center darkens and necroses, or dies, over hours to weeks. As the central dark area slowly spreads, it leaves an enlarging ulcer of dead tissue that may ultimately require skin grafting to repair.

In addition to the local signs of envenomation from a brown spider bite, generalized or *systemic* signs may also occur. These include fever, chills, rash, nausea, vomiting, malaise, weakness, bleeding, kidney failure, and fluid in the lungs (pulmonary edema). These effects are usually worse in children than in adults.

FIRST AID AND MEDICAL TREATMENT No specific first aid treatment has been shown to be helpful for *Loxosceles* bites. As with all bites or stings, washing the area with soap and water is recommended to help prevent infection. Anyone suspected of having a brown spider bite should seek medical evaluation, and anyone with severe signs of envenomation should be admitted to the hospital. Excising, or cutting out, the ulcerated area to remove the venom has not been shown to be helpful and may make the wound worse. There is currently no antivenom or other specific treatment available, although this is an area of active research.

Bark Scorpion (*Centruroides exilicauda*)
VENOMOUS

Range and habitat These small arthropods are found across southeastern California, southern and western Arizona, southern Nevada, extreme southeastern Utah, southwestern New Mexico, and south to Baja California and northern Sonora, Mexico. Exceptionally numerous in Arizona, they are frequently found in or near mesquite, cottonwood, and sycamore groves, and other riparian habitats—often on trees, under loose bark, and among rocks, stones, and leaf litter (particularly in washes), and in wood piles.

Diet Bark scorpions eat insects, spiders, and other arthropods, including other scorpions; occasionally small reptiles like geckos and lizards; and sometimes baby rodents.

Life span The juvenile mortality rate is high, but adults may live several years.

Physical characteristics The bark scorpion can be distinguished from other scorpions by a tail and pedipalps that appear longer and thinner than those of any other scorpion found in the United States. These are by far the most reliable field marks. The bark scorpion's chelae (pincer-like claws on the end of the pedipalps) are about six times longer than they are wide. Color and size are *not* specific for identification; like many other scorpions, bark scorpions are light

A bark scorpion under UV light (*Centruroides exilicauda*).

yellowish-tan or brown in color and about 2–3 inches (50–75 mm) in length (including the tail). The stinger of the bark scorpion is unique in having a tiny *tubercle* at the base, although this is virtually impossible to see on a living scorpion without picking it up and possibly getting stung in the process. The sternum, or breastplate, is long and not quite triangular (the bottom segment is curved), unlike the five-sided or pentagonal sternum of all other Southwest scorpion species. Lastly, unlike the similarly colored and similarly sized stripetail scorpion (*Vaejovis spinigerus*), the bark scorpion does not have stripes on the tail.

Behavior In contrast to essentially every other species of scorpion in the Southwest, bark scorpions are climbers, often found in trees and on the walls of houses or the banks of washes. They usually take cover during the day, hiding in darkness under rocks, bark, or debris, and come out on nights when the temperature is above approximately 77 degrees F (25 degrees C). They hibernate and are seldom seen in the winter, unless they have found the indoor warmth of a house. They defend individual territories, sometimes for days, although they will move at night in search of better hunting territory. Areas with ideal habitat are often home to hundreds of bark scorpions, often in close proximity to one another. They prefer moist areas and airflow—habitat that is frequently provided by a new home. When discovered in homes, they are often found on the walls or ceilings, trapped in a bathtub or shower stall, or clinging to sheets or towels, especially in dark closets and laundry or storage rooms.

Bark scorpions are generally not aggressive toward non-prey, unless threatened. Stings frequently occur when someone accidentally steps barefoot onto one, or in bed, when the scorpion is accidentally squeezed against the body under the sheets. When threatened, a bark scorpion will raise and curl its tail from a position parallel to the ground into a large arc over its head, with the point of the telson aiming forward. While holding onto the aggressor with its pedipalps if at all possible, it will sting, often repeatedly, with a flicking movement of the tail.

When hunting, a bark scorpion will lie in wait until prey comes within striking range, then lunge forward, grab the prey with its pedipalps and sting repeatedly, holding on until the prey is subdued. It will then pull the prey toward its mouth parts and chew and swallow until the prey item is gone.

Reproduction Bark scorpions have an elaborate courtship ritual that may last for several hours, in which they "dance" while the male holds onto the female's chelae with his own. The male deposits a *spermatophore,* or sperm package, on the ground and maneuvers the female until her genital opening is directly above it, allowing the sperm to be passed to the female. The female stores the sperm and later uses it to internally fertilize her eggs. The fertilized eggs will develop into small baby scorpions within the female. The young are born in the summer, and immediately climb up the mother's legs and pedipalps to her back, where she will carry them around until after their first molt. They gain independence as soon as they leave the back of the mother.

Effects of venom The venom of the bark scorpion is composed primarily of neurotoxins, and its stings are exceptionally painful and long-lasting. Children less than two years of age are particularly susceptible to the effects of this venom, which can be potentially life-threatening to this age group. Bark scorpion stings in children may cause progressive hyperactivity or restlessness, *nystagmus* (roving eyes), *ataxia* (loss of coordination), slurred speech, drooling, a thick tongue sensation, *hyperesthesia* (excessive sensitivity of the skin), muscle *fasciculations* (twitching), abdominal pain and cramps, and respiratory depression that requires mechanical ventilation. Death from scorpion envenomation in the United States is rare, and only seven deaths have been reported since 1970. Mexico is host to more toxic species of *Centruroides,* and scorpion stings in Mexico are responsible for about 100 deaths a year. This has led to a significant effort by Mexican pharmaceutical companies to develop an antivenom to scorpion toxins.

Envenomation from a bark scorpion usually causes little if any swelling or discoloration at the site of the sting, although an extremely severe stinging or burning sensation that radiates up an arm or leg is common. Tapping a finger on the area of the sting (the so-called "tap test") almost always causes extreme pain. The pain usually persists for 12 to 48 hours. In adults, systemic signs of envenomation and serious morbidity or mortality are rare.

FIRST AID AND MEDICAL TREATMENT If a young child is stung by a bark scorpion, medical care may be required within 15 minutes; therefore, a physician or poison center should be contacted immediately for assistance. Poison Center advice may also be useful for the medical management of older children and adults with stings.

Ice may be applied directly to the area of the sting, although the limb should not be soaked in ice water. Alcoholic beverages and sedatives should be avoided. Pain medication such as ibuprofen or acetaminophen may be taken, although prescription-strength narcotic pain medication may be required to control symptoms.

Children less than two years of age with severe symptoms are often treated in the hospital with intravenous valium-like drugs called benzodiazepines. Currently there is no FDA-approved antivenom available for scorpion stings, although FDA-approved clinical trials of Anascorp, an antivenom made in Mexico, are underway at many hospitals in Arizona.

Arizona Stripetail Scorpion or Devil Scorpion (*Vaejovis spinigerus*)
VENOMOUS

Range and habitat The Vaejovidae family's nine genera and more than 145 species are found across the United States and all of Mexico; they are found in nearly every habitat, from arid deserts to alpine mountains of southwestern Canada. The stripetail scorpion, *Vaejovis spinigerus,* is the most common species in Arizona, New Mexico, and southern California; stripetails can be found in or near washes, rocky outcroppings, riverbeds, and within houses. They are seldom found in sand dunes or in excessively sandy soil, contrary to popular belief.

Diet Stripetail scorpions eat insects, spiders, and other arthropods, including other scorpions.

Life span As with the bark scorpion, the juvenile mortality rate is high, but adults may live several years.

Physical characteristics Stripetail scorpions range in size up to about 2 inches (50 mm) in length, including the tail. They are light- or dark-brown or yellowish-tan in color. They can be distinguished from the similar-appearing bark scorpion by their much stockier appearance and the presence of a dark stripe on either side of the tail. The pincers and the tail segments are relatively short and fat, particularly when compared with those of the relatively sleek bark scorpion.

Behavior Stripetail scorpions are similar to bark scorpions, with a few significant differences. Stripetails are seldom found in trees, preferring to spend the daylight hours hidden under rocks or debris or within a burrow. Like bark scorpions, they are frequently found in homes, although they are usually discovered moving across the floor or in the pantry or laundry room, and less often on walls or the ceiling. Human encounters are often with bare feet, or on the fingers when someone unwittingly attempts to pick up a scorpion off the floor, mistaking it for a dust-ball or other debris.

Reproduction Stripetails, like other scorpions, have an elaborate courtship ritual lasting several hours, in which they "dance" while the male locks onto the female's chelae with his own. The male ultimately deposits a

Preventing scorpion stings

Most scorpion stings occur within or around the home, and many things can be done to reduce the likelihood of being stung:

- Woodpiles, old boards, rocks, and debris should be removed from areas immediately surrounding homes. Wear leather gloves when working with woodpiles or other debris.

- Seal doorways and other entrances to prevent scorpions form entering the home. Have your home inspected and sprayed for insects to prevent providing a "prey base" for scorpions.

- If scorpions are found inside the home, conduct a survey at night with a UV black light to look for them, and shake out bedding and towels before use. Infant cribs can be protected by setting the legs within wide-mouth glass jars, as scorpions are unable to climb clean glass. Make sure that everyone can recognize a scorpion and understands the danger of being stung.

spermatophore on the ground and maneuvers the female until her genital opening is directly above it; the female will temporarily store the sperm inside her body and will later use it to internally fertilize her eggs. Live young are born in the summer and immediately climb up the mother's legs and pedipalps to her back, where she will carry them around for 10 to 15 days, until after their first molt, when they gain independence. The number of young born depends on the size of the female and the availability of food and other resources—the larger the female and the more food available, the greater the number of young.

Effects of venom The venom of *Vaejovis* species is not nearly as toxic to humans as that of the bark scorpion. The pain of stripetail stings is not as severe, and symptoms usually last for up to several hours, rather than days. Those who have been stung compare the experience to that of a bee sting. The stings are generally not considered life-threatening, even in children.

FIRST AID AND MEDICAL TREATMENT As with all bites and stings, the area should be washed with soap and water. An ice cube can be applied to the affected area and ibuprofen

or acetaminophen taken for pain relief. For atypical reactions, consult with your physician or a poison center.

Giant Hairy Scorpion or Giant Hairy Desert Scorpion (*Hadrurus arizonensis*)
VENOMOUS

Range and habitat *H. arizonensis* lives in arid regions of Arizona, as well as southern parts of California, Utah, and Nevada. They may be found under logs or rock piles in gardens and around homes, especially in areas with high moisture content or where lights attract insects; other habitat includes washes and open desert. They may rest in burrows up to 8 inches (25 cm) deep, where relative humidity remains high.

Diet They eat insects, spiders, and other arthropods, including other scorpions, and may also occasionally feed on small reptiles like geckos and lizards.

Life span Most likely lives several years; capable of surviving cold winters by burrowing and changing its metabolism into a "winter" mode analogous to hibernation.

Physical characteristics This is by far the largest scorpion in the United States, with some specimens reaching a length of up to 6 inches (15 cm). The overall color is yellow-tan, with dark brown covering most of the top of the cephalothorax and abdomen. The name derives from the overall size and the small "hairs" that cover the extremities and tail, including the telson. The hairs are thought to serve in a sensory capacity.

Behavior The giant hairy scorpion is the least frequently encountered of the three common species of scorpion in the Southwest, although it is by far the most impressive. It prefers to hide in underground burrows when not foraging at night. Giant hairy scorpions are seldom, if ever, found within homes, but they may be uncovered in gardens under rocks or planters, or discovered at night foraging.

Reproduction The courtship ritual of giant hairy scorpions is similar to that of the stripetail and bark scorpions. The male locks onto the female's chelae with his own, and the pair "dance" until the male deposits a spermatophore (sperm package) on the ground and then maneuvers the female's genital opening directly above it, allowing the sperm to be passed to the female. The female will temporarily store the sperm and later use it to internally fertilize her eggs. Live young are born in the summer and immediately climb onto the mother's back, where she will carry them around for about 20 days until after their first molt, when they disperse. The young scorpions will molt seven times during their first year of life, before they reach adulthood.

Effects of venom Fortunately, the toxicity of the venom of the giant hairy scorpion is not proportional to its size. Most of those who have been stung by this scorpion state that the pain is initially intense, but that it quickly resolves, often within 5 to 20 minutes. Interestingly, a new antimicrobial peptide called hadrurin has been isolated from the venom of a very similar species of Mexican scorpion, *Hadrurus aztecus*. It is not yet known if this peptide exists in the venom of the giant hairy scorpion, or why a peptide with antimicrobial properties even exists within a scorpion venom.

FIRST AID AND MEDICAL TREATMENT As with all bites and stings, wash the affected area with soap and water. To reduce pain, an ice cube can be held against the skin where the sting occurred. Both ibuprofen and acetaminophen can be taken for pain. For atypical or serious reactions, consult with your physician or a poison center.

Giant Vinegaroon, Vinegaroon, or Whip Scorpion (*Mastigoproctus giganteus*)
NON-VENOMOUS

Range and habitat Vinegaroons live in the southern United States and in Mexico; they are typically found in burrows under logs, rocks, or other natural debris, or even sometimes indoors in humid dark corners or basements.

Diet Like most other arachnids, vinegaroons are predatory and eat crickets and other insects.

Life span Unknown, but thought to be several years.

Physical characteristics The vinegaroon looks like a large black scorpion, with its huge pedipalps and chelae and segmented body, but the astute observer will quickly notice that this 3–6-inch (7–15 cm, total length) arachnid lacks a segmented tail, and there is no telson, or stinging apparatus. This non-venomous look-alike can spray an irritating vinegar-like solution containing acetic acid from two

Reproduction Vinegaroon courtship is similar to that of the scorpions, except that after mating the female carries her fertilized eggs in a sac. After hatching, the babies ride on their mother's back for several days to weeks, similar to scorpions.

Windscorpions, Sopulgids, or Sun Spiders
(*Eremobates* and *Ammotrechidae* species)
NON-VENOMOUS

Range and habitat These arthropods are found in the hottest, driest deserts of the world, as well as in tropical areas; more than 50 species occur in the southwestern United States. Their natural habitat includes dry riverbeds, washes, and abandoned rodent burrows, and are also found in or around houses.

Diet Windscorpions eat insects and occasionally very small vertebrate animals, such as lizards.

Life span Unknown, but probably several years.

Physical characteristics Solpugids (as these arachnids are sometimes called, after their order, Solpugidae, or more recently, Solifugidae) look like spiders, although they are neither spiders nor scorpions. They are yellow-brown, with four pairs of legs and a long, modified pair of pedipalps that look like a fifth pair of legs or antennae, and

organs at the base of the flagellum, or tail (but not through the tip of the tail); the tail is used as a sensory appendage. The first of the four pairs of legs look like long antennae and are also modified to serve in a sensory capacity.

Behavior Vinegaroons are active at night and hide under rocks, leaves, or wood during the day; they feed on crickets and other insects. Contrary to their dangerous appearance, they neither bite nor sting.

enormous chelicerae or mouth parts that project forward like pincers. Unlike spiders, but similar to scorpions, their abdomens are segmented. The Solpugid species of the Southwest are about ⅜ to 1 inch (10–25 mm) in length at maximum (Solpugids in the Middle East are much larger). Males remain smaller than females, and their legs are longer in proportion to body length.

Behavior Sopulgids are often called windscorpions for the incredible speed at which they run. They have a powerful, painful bite, and although at one time they were considered venomous, their poison glands are not associated with their mouth parts, and they do not cause serious envenomation symptoms in humans. Solpugids are solitary, independent hunters.

Reproduction After mating, the female digs out an area in the soil, then hides her eggs there and stands guard until they hatch. Young are primarily nocturnal, venturing about in daylight only after they approach adult size.

MYRIAPODS

Centipedes and millipedes fall within a subdivision or *superclass* of arthropods called Myriapoda, which not surprisingly means "with many feet." Myriapods are among the oldest lineages of the arthropods, and paleontological data traces them back to the Cambrian period, some 490–543 million years ago. All 13,000 species of myriapods are terrestrial and prefer to live in humid or moist environments, under leaf litter or other debris such as wood or rock; most are nocturnal. Every myriapod has a head with a single pair of antennae, a maxilla or upper jaw, and one or two mandibles or lower jaws, as well as an elongated, segmented trunk with many legs. Myriapods are subdivided into chilopods, diplopods, and two lesser-known classes called symphylans and pauropods, which superficially resemble tiny centipedes.

The chilopods, or centipedes, are mostly predatory and can be easily identified by their single pair of legs per body segment. They also have a pair of maxillapeds, or jaw-feet, that are modified into venomous claws or fangs, allowing the larger centipedes to subdue prey such as frogs and mice. Centipedes may typically live 1 to 6 years.

The diplopods, or **millipedes,** have fused double-trunk segments that give the appearance of two pairs of walking legs per body segment. They primarily feed on both living and decaying plant material and do not bite or have a venom-delivery mechanism, although some can release a noxious odor. They may live up to 10 years.

Giant Desert Centipede (*Scolopendra heros*)
VENOMOUS

Range and habitat Giant desert centipedes are found throughout the southwestern U.S. and much of Mexico, particularly in arid desert regions. They frequently burrow underground or hide during the day in rock piles or in attics and crawl spaces in houses; they prefer damp environments, and may be found near (or in!) swimming pools and under logs or rocks in areas that are watered frequently or where the relative humidity is high.

Diet Giant desert centipedes eat insects, other arthropods, slugs, worms, geckos and other lizards, and small snakes, as well as small or newborn rodents.

Life span May live for many years in captivity; life span in the wild is unknown, but they require several years to attain sexual maturity.

Physical characteristics The giant desert centipede may reach 6 to 8 inches in length (15–22 cm). At first glance, it may be difficult to tell which end is the head and which is the tail, as the last pair of legs are modified in shape and color to resemble the antennae (and so the last segment is sometimes referred to as a *pseudohead*). These long hind legs are often used to help hold prey. Like other centipedes, giant desert centipedes have one pair of legs per body segment, and the total number of pairs of legs in this species is 21. An additional first pair of legs is adapted to form the *gnathosomes,* or pincer-like claws or fangs that are connected to a venom apparatus. As the gnathosomes are derived from legs and not mouth parts, there has been debate as to whether the giant

desert centipede bites or stings. Regardless of the semantics, the parts that inject venom are near the mouth end, not the tail end. The color of *Scolopendra heros* is variable, although the body is often a dark yellow-orange-tan color with black bands, and contrasts with the head and last pair of legs, which are often orange or red.

Behavior The giant desert centipede is loath to be caught in the light, and if so exposed, will quickly run in any direction for cover, including up nearby pant legs. This nocturnal predator is very active and very fast, and also very quick to bite if handled. Most bites occur accidentally while a victim is putting on clothes or while in bed. The centipede may bite repeatedly or tenaciously if trapped, as in a pant leg.

Reproduction The reproduction of the giant desert centipede is not unlike that of many other arthropods. Mating begins with a "head-to-tail" coupling of the male and female, who dance in a circle for an hour or more. The male will ultimately construct a spermatophore using silk from glands on his underside, and he will drop the spermatophore and maneuver the female until she is directly over it and picks it up. After fertilization, the female will lay eggs in old, decayed wood or cactus and will stay with the eggs and defend them until several days after they hatch.

Effects of venom The bite of the giant desert centipede is very painful, but it is not considered particularly dangerous to either adults or children. The venom causes both pain and swelling, and often red streaking called *lymphangitis*. There may be systemic symptoms including anxiety, fever, dizziness, palpitations, and nausea. Skin breakdown may occur at the site of a bite, but it usually heals without the need for skin grafting or other medical treatment. Rarely, the envenomation can cause extensive muscle breakdown that can lead to dangerous swelling in a limb or to kidney failure. There have been no known fatalities due to giant desert centipede envenomations.

FIRST AID AND MEDICAL TREATMENT The mainstay of treatment of centipede bites is good wound care and the treatment of pain. As with all bites and stings, the area should be washed with soap and water. Heat applied to the area may provide some relief. Ibuprofen or acetaminophen may be taken for pain relief. For atypical reactions, or for pain that cannot be controlled with these treatments, consult your physician or a poison center.

Desert Millipede (*Orthoporus ornatus*)
NON-VENOMOUS

Range and habitat Desert millipedes' range includes west Texas, southern New Mexico, and southeastern Arizona, as well parts of Colorado and Oklahoma; the southern end of their range extends to Sonora and Chihuahua, Mexico. Preferred habitat includes dry lowlands and, more frequently, higher-elevation grasslands.

Diet These herbivores or detritivores feed on both living and decaying plant material.

Life span Typically lives 4–8 years.

Physical characteristics Contrary to their name, millipedes don't have a million legs, or even a thousand. Although they look similar to centipedes, they have two pairs of walking legs on almost every body segment, rather than one, and

they don't bite. Although there are about 7,500 species of millipedes, the type most frequently encountered in the Southwest is the large, reddish-brown desert millipede. Depending on the species, millipedes vary in size from a fraction of an inch in length to about 9 inches (23 cm). The long, cylindrical body has a hard exoskeleton, and there is a short pair of antennae on the head.

Behavior Millipedes are mostly nocturnal, but are sometimes seen during the day, especially after periods of heavy rainfall. In some areas of their range, particularly when it is humid, their population density can be extremely high, making them one of the most commonly encountered invertebrates. During hot, dry weather, millipedes are at risk of desiccation, and activity is severely curtailed. Adults overwinter and become active during the spring. Millipedes move with a strong wave-like motion of their legs. When threatened, they curl up into a ball to protect the softer, more vulnerable underside. They may also emit a brown liquid with a foul odor as a defense mechanism.

Reproduction Young are born during the spring, and after approximately 21 to 25 weeks and seven *instars* (the developmental stages between each molt) they develop into adults. During this period, they continue to add leg-bearing body segments.

INSECTS

Bees, wasps, ants, and even caterpillars—sometimes it seems that everything with more than four legs stings! Fortunately, most insects don't sting, and most insect venoms are not particularly dangerous to people. The greatest risk that we face from insect stings is anaphylaxis—a severe allergic reaction that can be triggered by even minute amounts of proteins in a venom. Anaphylaxis is most common in people who have been sensitized to the protein that triggers the reaction, usually by previous exposure from a sting. Given the tremendous diversity of insects and relatively low medical risk from most insect stings, this book covers only a few of the more significant members of this class.

Insects are a class of arthropods that have three main body sections: head, thorax, and abdomen. They have three pairs of legs attached to the thorax, and usually two sets of wings. The insect life cycle is either three-part (egg, nymph, adult) or four-part (egg, larva, pupa, adult). Insects account for most of the biomass on earth and are represented by over a million *known* species, divided into 32 orders; it is thought that there may be as many as 10 million species. The most recently discovered order of insects are the Mantophasmatodea, or "gladiators," that were described in Namibia in 2002.

Harvester Ants (*Pogonomyrmex* species)
VENOMOUS

Range and habitat Harvester ants are found across the Southwest. Their colonies are generally constructed in flat areas, with the main opening to the colony centered within a 3- to 6-foot-wide circle (about 1–2 m) where the ants have cleared the vegetation; a small "crater" of pebbles immediately surrounds the opening. Harvester ants do not invade homes.

Diet These ants survive on seeds, collected and brought underground to the colony, where they are treated with antibiotic saliva and stored (the saliva helps prevent the seed from decomposing); the ants rotate stores of seeds to prevent spoilage.

Life span A mature colony may live for many years. Queens live over five years; males live less than a year and die within hours or days of leaving the colony.

Physical characteristics There are about 11 species of harvester ants in the Southwest. All belong to the genus *Pogonomyrmex,* giving rise to the nickname pogo ants, or pogos. Harvester ants range in size from about ⅕ to ⅜ inch (5–10 mm) in length, and they may be red, dark brown, or black in color. They have large mandibles and long hairs on the underside of the head called *psammophores.* All ants have a long, thin connection between the thorax and abdomen called a "petiole" that has one or two bumps on it, and antennae with a single joint in the middle. These characteristics distinguish them from termites, bees, and wasps. Like bees and wasps, female ants have stingers on the end of the abdomen, and they can both sting and bite. A colony consists of a queen, winged males, and workers, and all vary in size, with the queen being the largest. There may be several sizes of workers (non-reproductive females), depending on the species and their function within the colony.

Behavior Harvester ants build enormous underground colonies that may extend more than 21 feet (nearly 7 meters) deep. The surface openings of the colony are usually in sunny areas that have been cleared of vegetation, and most species of harvester ants build craters of sand that surround the opening holes. The ants bring the excavated sand to the surface by holding pieces in their large, powerful mandibles. Small, fine sand is carried out in the psammophores, which function like an under-the-chin shovel. Frequently, several ants can be seen cooperating to get a large piece of sand out of the opening hole and up and over the top of the surrounding crater, where they let it fall down and roll away. Sometimes several ants will attach to and pull on the same rock, and at other times several ants will hold on to and pull another ant that is holding the rock, like one side of a miniature tug-of-war.

If resources become scarce or if conditions around the colony become unfavorable, the colony is capable of quickly moving to another location, transporting eggs, pupae, and food supplies with them.

Harvester ants have few natural predators other than horned lizards ("horned toads"), which feed on them and seem impervious to the stings.

Reproduction When a colony is thriving, winged males and females called *alates* are produced. The alates stay within the colony until favorable external conditions—usually summer rains—trigger them to emerge and seek mates from other colonies. Large swarms of alates are cast off from the colony all at once, yet the reproductive success of the females is low, with perhaps one out of 500 surviving to start a new colony. New colonies are initiated by the mating of winged male and female ants. The male dies soon after mating; the female removes her own wings by pushing them forward with her legs until they detach, then she finds or excavates a place to lay eggs. The eggs that hatch usually become non-reproductive females, or workers, that assist with excavation of the colony, care of the eggs and pupae, foraging for seed, and defense of the colony.

Effects of venom Harvester ants can both bite and sting. To sting, the ant first bites onto the skin, then arches its back and drives its stinger into the tented-up skin that it is biting. The stinger is not barbed, and the ant may sting repeatedly while biting and holding on. With a secure bite, it swivels its body around in a semi-circle, stinging repeatedly, with the stings forming an arc around the bite. There is often a delay of five to 30 seconds before the onset of the intense pain from the stings, which lasts about four to six hours. The stings often cause a purple, bruised area around the site, followed by blistering and inflammation. Other symptoms may include nausea, vomiting, and shooting pains (paresthesias) from the location of the stings, lasting about 24 hours.

The venom from the pogo ant is the most toxic insect venom known. Studies have shown that about 12 stings can

The world of ants

Roughly 9,500 ant species inhabit the earth, and these social insects make up 10 percent of the biomass of the world—and 30 percent of the biomass of the Amazon. Like bees, ants are social insects that live in complex colonies of thousands of individuals. They are highly evolved and have become very specialized, falling into several broad categories defined by their behavior. For example, leafcutter ants cut leaves to grow fungus; army ants march in columns and conduct daily raids, devouring anything edible in their path; harvester ants collect and store huge quantities of seeds underground; and weaver ants, a fascinating arboreal type, use the silk from larval ants to glue tree leaves together to build a nest. There are even slave-making ants that capture pupae from other ant species and use the ants that emerge as workers!

A winged male harvester ant (*Pogonomyrmex* sp.).

kill a 4.4-pound (2 kg) rat. The venom of a single South-western harvester ant, *Pogonomyrmex maricopa,* is more than 20 times more lethal than honeybee venom when tested in mice. Interestingly, harvester ant venoms are more than 100 times more toxic to mammals than to arthro-pods, suggesting that this venom has evolved as a defense against mammals.

Harvester ant venom contains toxins that make it sim-ilar to many bee venoms (but unlike fire ant venom). The toxins in harvester ant venom—phospholipase A2 and B, lipase, and hyaluronidase, among others—break down cell walls and make the cells die. Hemolysin in the venom makes red blood cells rupture and is responsible for the purple bruised-appearing area around the sting. Many of the components of harvester ant venom are capable of inducing allergic reactions, including anaphylaxis.

FIRST AID AND MEDICAL TREATMENT People are usually stung by ants when they unknowingly encounter a colony or one of its trails of workers. The workers near the colony may be very aggressive, particularly near the time that colonies swarm and release alates. Children who do not recognize the risk of an ant colony, or those who go bare-foot or wear sandals or sleep on the ground, are most at risk. It's also obvious that you should be careful where you spread your picnic blanket or put down your sleeping bag.

Before beginning first aid, remove the victim from the area and kill or remove any remaining ants. Unless there is a severe reaction, a large number of stings, or the pain is intolerable, medical care is usually not needed. The area should be washed with soap and water, and ice may be applied. Acetaminophen or ibuprofen may be taken for pain. Benadryl (taken orally every four hours) may help decrease itching and allergic symptoms like localized redness and swelling.

Africanized Honeybees (*Apis mellifera*)
VENOMOUS

Range and habitat These aggressive bees are currently found across the Southwest, from Texas through southern California, north into southern Nevada and parts of Oklahoma, and eastward as far as Alabama. They are also found throughout Mexico. Their preferred habitat includes areas with flowering plants and a source of water; hives are often constructed within enclosed areas that remain relatively cool, such as tree cavities, walls or attics, and electrical boxes.

Diet Honeybees dine on flower nectar, pollen, and honey.

Life span Queens live 3 to 5 years; drones live 5 to 10 weeks, dying shortly after mating (unmated drones are denied food from the colony and quickly die); worker bees live about 50 days, although many die off more quickly in winter .

Physical characteristics Africanized bees look nearly identical to our common European-derived honeybees, and the two can be physically differentiated only by experts, using microscopic analysis of the wings or DNA tests. There are very few traits that can be identified by eye—whereas in the lab, more than 20 different structures are measured and compared.

Queens are about ¾ inch (18–20 mm), drones (males, whose role in life is to reproduce) are about ⅝ inch (15–17 mm), and sterile female workers are about ⅜–⅝ inch long (10–15 mm). The drones have large compound eyes, and

the queen has small compound eyes; those of the worker bees fall in the middle. The head, antennae, and legs are black, other body parts are reddish-brown, and there are orange rings on the abdomen. There is a pollen basket on the hind legs. The wings are clear. The stinger is highly barbed, and after stinging, it gets pulled out of the body of the bee and remains in the victim. The stinger contains a muscular "pump" and valve that injects venom into a victim after a sting.

Behavior The social structure of a bee colony is centered on maintaining the health of the queen and the colony. This is even more apparent in Africanized bees than in our European-derived honeybee colonies.

Africanized bees are very defensive and easily agitated. Non-Africanized bees often take up to 30 seconds to respond to a perceived threat to the hive, whereas Africanized bees will respond within 3 seconds. They do so with overwhelming force, often sending 10 times the number of

Africanized bee migration

All honeybees in the Americas are descendants of European bees brought to America with the early settlers. Africanized honeybees, commonly called "killer bees," are the product of good science gone bad. They are recent immigrants, feared for their aggressiveness and their potential to kill. In 1956, Brazilian scientists were breeding African bees with local European bees to make better hybrids for the tropics. Some of what turned out to be very aggressive Africanized hybrids escaped, and wild colonies have been moving north ever since, at a rate of about 250–350 miles per year. Unfortunately, in addition to being exceptionally aggressive, these hybrid bees produce only about one-fifth of the honey that non-hybrid bees make.

Africanized bees first entered the U.S. in 1990, and the first Africanized bee attack in the United States occurred in Brownsville, Texas, in 1991. Africanized bees were discovered in Arizona and New Mexico in 1993, the same year that the first fatalities occurred in the United States. To date, Mexico has had hundreds of fatalities from Africanized bee attacks, and as of April 2005, 15 fatalities in the U.S. have been attributed to Africanized bee stings. Far greater numbers of dogs and other animals have been killed.

Victims who die from Africanized bee attacks are most often old or frail, or otherwise have difficulty getting away. Dogs are also frequent victims, and even a healthy horse was attacked and killed after children threw rocks at an Africanized beehive and unleashed their fury.

A swarm of Africanized bees resting in a mesquite tree.

soldier bees as would a non-Africanized bee colony. Like drug-crazed psychopaths, Africanized bees will pursue victims for up to a quarter of a mile (.4 km), whereas non-Africanized bees will stop pursuit after about 25–30 yards (23–27 meters). The unfortunate victim of such an attack is likely to receive far greater than ten times the number of stings from an Africanized bee attack compared with what would be received from a typical bee attack.

Preventing bee attacks

The danger in Africanized bee attacks lies not in a difference in the venom, but in the number of stings a victim receives. Therefore, the immediate priority during an attack is to get to a sheltered area such as a building or vehicle as quickly as possible. The head and face in particular should be covered, even if this results in more stings to another body area. If there is not a protected area nearby, run in a straight line as fast and far as possible, and do not run toward other people or you may involve them in the attack as well. Bees do not fly fast and it is possible to outrun them. Jumping into water is not considered a safe retreat, as the bees will wait until a person surfaces and then sting the head en masse.

Not becoming the target of an attack is preferable to surviving an attack. Swatting at even single bees near a hive can induce a colony to attack, as can loud noises or vibrations like car engines or yard equipment. Dark colors seem to attract attacking bees far more so than light colors, and some perfumes and aftershaves are known to stimulate attacks. Isoamyl acetate, a component of banana oil, is an attack pheromone produced by bees to signal others to join an attack, so don't eat your ripe banana near a hive.

After Africanized bees become agitated, they frequently need a day or two to calm down. This compares with the several hours needed for non-Africanized bees. Africanized bees also tend to swarm more, and when resources dwindle, Africanized bees are more likely to pack up their honey reserves and begin to migrate, re-establishing the colony in an area with better resources. They also produce more drones (males), and those drones out-compete non-Africanized drones for mating, thus introducing their genes into more colonies. These combined traits have been responsible for the rapid northward spread of Africanized bees.

Away from the hive, Africanized bees are no more aggressive than other honeybees. They do not form large swarms to hunt for people or animals, as shown in popular movies. Worker bees collect pollen and nectar and maintain the honeycombed wax hive. Soldier bees protect the colony and the queen.

In spring, about half the workers from a colony will split off and swarm, looking for a new location to start a colony. Swarming bees are generally not overly aggressive, and they usually move on after several days to a week at a given resting site.

Reproduction The honeybee life cycle is complex. Queen bees are able to store sperm after mating, and only fertilized eggs laid by the queen will turn into worker bees. Unfertilized eggs turn into drones (males). A queen will lay sufficient eggs over time to produce a colony of 60,000 to 80,000 worker bees.

A queen bee in an established colony will lay about 1,500 to 1,900 eggs in a single day (mostly during summer, totaling about 200,000 eggs a year), depositing each egg into an empty cell in the honeycomb. The eggs hatch into legless, wingless larvae in three days, which are fed by "nurse bees." The larvae will molt through five instars during the six days after hatching, then the cell is capped by workers and each larva spins a cocoon. After eight to ten days the cocoon hatches into an adult bee.

If something happens to the queen, or if the colony is about to swarm, nurse bees produce "royal jelly" to feed to newly hatched larvae. This will predispose them to become queens, but it only works if they are fed royal jelly before they are three days old.

Effects of venom   Bee venom is perhaps the most thoroughly investigated animal venom. It consists of several components, including enzymes, peptides, and histamine. The enzymes are responsible for the breakdown of cell walls, allowing the venom to spread. Of the peptides in bee venom, mellitin is the most important. This 26-amino-acid string joins with three other mellitin peptides to form a tetramer. The tetramer is shaped like a tunnel or channel, and it acts as an *ionophore* to form holes in the cell walls of the nerve cells that are responsible for pain signals. The passage of sodium and potassium through the mellitin channels causes the nerve cells to fire repeatedly, sending pain signals to the brain. There are many other minor components of the venom, any of which can trigger an allergic reaction.

FIRST AID AND MEDICAL TREATMENT   After a bee sting (or stings), the stinger(s) should be removed immediately, even by pinching the stinger and pulling it out. A previously recommended method of removing stingers was to scrape the stinger out with a card or flat object to avoid squeezing venom out of the sting. Research has shown that this is not necessary and often delays removal. The sting has a valve mechanism, and squeezing the sting does not cause more venom to be released. Most of the venom will be pumped into the victim within 30 seconds by the muscular stinging apparatus, therefore the more quickly the stinger is removed, the better.

Preliminary data indicates that the number of stings a healthy individual receives will determine the likely outcome. Victims who receive more than ten stings per pound of body weight will likely die. Those who receive less than four stings per pound of body weight will likely survive. Clearly, minimizing the number of stings is the key to survival.

Many people are highly allergic to bee stings and experience anaphylaxis after being stung. For these people, an epinephrine self-injector (Epi-Pen) can be lifesaving, as even a single sting could be fatal.

Anyone experiencing a severe reaction after being stung should seek prompt medical evaluation and treatment. Ice can be applied to the areas that have been stung, and acetaminophen or ibuprofen may be taken for pain. Benadryl may help treat localized allergic symptoms such as itching or rash.

Tarantula Hawk (*Pepsis* species)
VENOMOUS

Range and habitat Tarantula hawks live wherever tarantulas are found: across Texas, New Mexico, Arizona, and California, with their upper range extending to southern Utah, and south into Mexico. Preferred habitat includes any area with tarantulas that also includes a good nectar source; dry hills with flowering shrubs are favored, along with flowering plants in back yards.

Diet Adults feed on pollen and nectar; larvae feed on tarantulas.

Life span Unknown.

Physical characteristics The largest wasps found in the Southwest are the tarantula hawks, members of the Pompilidae or spiderwasp family, all of which prey on specific spiders. Over 250 species of tarantula hawks occur in North and Central America, with roughly 12 of the 15 species found in the U.S. occurring in the Southwest. Species identification is difficult. These wasps are capable of delivering the most painful sting of any North American insect—far more painful than that of the honeybee. The most impressive physical characteristic of tarantula hawks is their size. Their bodies may be over 2 inches long, and are usually a "gunmetal blue" or black color, often with hints of iridescence. There is a short "waist" (pedicle) between the thorax

and abdomen. Males generally have longer, straighter antennae than the short, strongly curved antennae found on females. The large wings are frequently bright orange or red, although a few species have black ones. The bright color of the wings is thought to serve as a warning to potential predators and is referred to as *aposematic* coloring. Few animals have an appetite (or the nerve!) for tarantula hawks, with the notable exception of the roadrunner.

Behavior Although tarantula hawks are most often seen feeding on flowering plants in the summer, they get their name from the manner in which the females hunt for prey for their offspring. Male tarantula hawks, on the other hand, do not hunt. In fact, because the stinger of wasps is actually a modified ovipositor, male tarantula hawks do not have stingers and are harmless.

Tarantula hawks are generally not aggressive unless threatened or disturbed.

Reproduction Mating takes place on or near flowering plants. After mating, female wasps will cruise over the desert ground, looking for tarantula holes, perhaps aided by their keen sense of smell. On finding a likely burrow, the wasp will entice the spider to come out, often by vibrating the silk strands at the entrance, imitating ensnared prey. If the tarantula emerges, the tarantula hawk quickly stings it in one of the nerve centers called ganglia at the base of a leg. The injected venom paralyzes the spider. The wasp lays one egg on the spider and buries the tarantula within its own hole or drags it off to another nearby hole, pushing it in and then sealing the opening. The wasp larva will feed on the paralyzed spider for months, then pupate until the following spring, when an adult wasp will emerge.

Effects of venom Although incredibly painful, the sting of the tarantula hawk is usually not particularly dangerous, although the death of a child from such a sting has been reported. Studies have shown that on a pain scale ranging from 0 to 4, with 4 being the most painful, the sting of the tarantula hawk rates a 4, while for comparison that of the fire ant rates a 1, the honeybee rates a 2, and the velvet ant (actually a wasp) rates a 3. Stings from tarantula hawks have left people lying on the ground, screaming in agony. Fortunately, the duration of the pain is usually only about three to five minutes. Perhaps the only insect that can match the pain induced by the sting of the tarantula hawk is the bullet ant (*Paraponera clavata*) in South America.

Little is known about the venom of the tarantula hawk, including what toxins are present or how they work.

FIRST AID AND MEDICAL TREATMENT As with all bites and sting, the area should be washed with soap and water. No further medical care is usually needed, especially given the short duration of the pain caused by the sting, unless the victim is a child or shows signs of an allergic reaction (hives, tongue or lip swelling, difficulty breathing, etc.) or if the symptoms persist for more than a few minutes.

Cone-nose or Kissing Bug (*Triatoma* species)
NON-VENOMOUS

Range and habitat Cone-nose bugs range throughout the U.S., with six species specific to the Southwest; preferred habitat includes packrat middens and the burrows of other mammals, although they are also often found in homes.

Diet These bloodsuckers are usually parasitic on wood rats, packrats, and other mammals, including people.

Life span Unknown.

Physical characteristics The six species of the cone-nose bug in the Southwest differ slightly in coloration. They

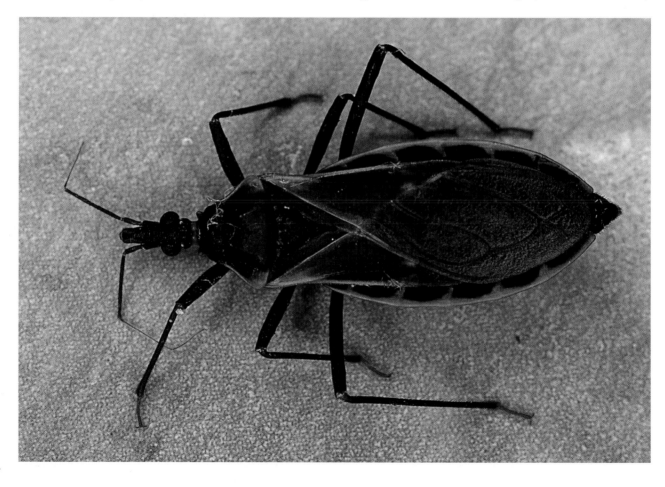

range in length from about ⅜ inch to just over 1 inch (1–3 cm), and they usually have red or orange markings at the edges of their brown or black wings. These flattened insects have elongated, cone-shaped heads bearing a pair of antennae, each with five to six segments, and a prominent beak or *proboscis*.

Behavior Although they most commonly feed on packrats' blood, kissing bugs are not very selective and will readily feed on a human host, often while the host is asleep. Kissing bug bites are painless and often last for 10–20 minutes. During the bite, they inject saliva containing an anticoagulant to keep the blood from clotting. About 5 percent of people who are bitten by these insects develop an allergy to the proteins in the saliva, and they may experience symptoms as severe as anaphylaxis after a bite. For most people, the bite of the kissing bug leaves a large welt that can last for hours or days but causes no other problems. Rarely in the U.S., but not uncommonly in Mexico and further south, these blood-sucking bugs may transmit a spirochete bacteria in their saliva that causes Chagas disease, which primarily affects the heart.

Reproduction The female kissing bug lays individual pearly white subconical eggs in a habitat near its food source. These eggs hatch in 10 to 30 days into small soft-bodied nymphs (similar in shape to adults but smaller and lacking wings). There are five nymphal stages, each requiring at least one full blood meal to stimulate molting to the next

growth stage. Completion of growth from egg to adult usually takes 1–2 years.

Buckmoth Caterpillars (*Hemileuca* species)
VENOMOUS

Range and habitat Various *Hemileuca* species are found across southern Arizona, New Mexico, and Texas, and south through Sonora and Chihuahua, Mexico; habitat varies from mesquite bosques to grasslands and plains, depending on the species.

Diet Common hosts in the Southwest include palo verde, mesquite, and other desert thornscrub trees, depending on the species of *Hemileuca*.

Life span Life span of the moth is likely less than a year; caterpillar phase lasts about a month.

Physical characteristics A number of caterpillars have developed an effective form of chemical defense that utilizes "stinging spines" on their bodies to ward off would-be predators. The most common of these are the buckmoth caterpillars, of which about 23 species are found in the Southwest. The full-grown caterpillars are about 2 inches long (5 cm) and are covered from one end to the other with bristles or *urticating* spines. The colors are variable and depend on the species.

The fast-flying adult moths have a wingspan of about 2–3 inches (5–7.5 cm), and vary in color from relatively nondescript tan and brown to brilliantly colored yellow and orange on black. They are primarily day-fliers, and they do not have stinging spines.

Behavior Juno buckmoth caterpillars feed on the leaves of common desert trees, often in groups. When molested, the caterpillar usually stops feeding and remains motionless, counting on camouflage and the urticating spines for protection. Caterpillars occasionally drop off branches and land on people, or are brushed against by riders on horseback, resulting in envenomation by the urticating spines. Other buckmoth caterpillars, like those of the range caterpillar moth (*Hemileuca oliviae*), feed on grasses, and envenomations can inadvertently occur when a person is walking through the grass.

Reproduction The life cycle of moths is somewhat complex, and the particular details are species-specific. Flights generally occur from September through December. The mating of most *Hemileuca* moths, such as the Juno or mesquite buckmoth (*Hemileuca juno*), begins shortly after sunset on fall evenings. Males use their well-developed antennae to track and follow the pheromone trail given off by female moths. After mating, the female deposits eggs on branches in host trees, with the eggs usually laid in circles around small branches. The eggs over-winter and hatch in April or May into small larvae, or caterpillars, that eat and grow for about a month, molting through five instars before they migrate to the ground and form a pupa, or cocoon, in leaf litter. After metamorphosis, most of the cocoons will hatch into adults (in the fall again), although some *Hemileuca* cocoons have been known to lie dormant for four years.

Effects of venom The spines of stinging caterpillars contain toxins that are produced in gland cells. Caterpillars do not have a stinging apparatus per se, but rather depend on intentional or inadvertent contact of the spines with the skin of a victim. After the spines penetrate the skin, they break off, releasing toxins that cause mild to severe pain and other compounds that induce an inflammatory dermatitis called *erucism*. Because the protein components of the toxins are considered "foreign" to the body, an allergic reaction may also occur. While hospitalization is rarely required for stings on the skin, spines that enter the eyes may cause potentially serious complications.

FIRST AID AND MEDICAL TREATMENT Anyone attempting to remove a stinging caterpillar should be careful not to incur additional stings on the hands or elsewhere, particularly as the caterpillar drops off. Wash the area immediately with soap and water. Spines that remain in the skin can often be removed with adhesive tape. Baking soda applied as a paste with water may help decrease the pain, as may ice applied to the injured area. Acetaminophen or ibuprofen may be taken for pain. Benadryl® may help treat localized allergic reactions. As always, victims with severe allergic reactions should seek immediate medical attention, as should anyone with persistent symptoms or signs of infection.

Amphibians

Amphibians are cold-blooded vertebrates with smooth skins; they hatch as aquatic larvae with gills, then transform into air-breathing adults with lungs. The class Amphibia includes frogs, toads, salamanders, and newts, and most are capable of living on land or in water. There are nearly 5,000 species of amphibians worldwide, and a significant number of these are poisonous, such as the well-known poison arrow frogs of Central and South America. The poisons in amphibians are usually found in the skin or skin secretions.

Frogs and toads are subdivided within the class Amphibians into an order called the Anura. Of the amphibians in the United States, only two species of toad (*Bufo marinus* and *Bufo alvarius*) and the roughskin newt (*Taricha granulose*) are considered poisonous and potentially dangerous. The roughskin newt is found along the west coast of the United States from Alaska to central California, but not in the Southwest.

TOADS

Although nearly everyone "knows one when they see one," the term "toad" has little taxonomic usefulness, even though it is still commonly used to describe the anurans that are not frogs. The two poisonous species of toads in the United States are both members of the large family of "true toads" called Bufonidae. The giant toad (also called the marine toad or cane toad), *Bufo marinus,* is native to Texas (but is endangered and rarely seen there) and is not otherwise found in the Southwest; it *is* found in Florida, however, where it was introduced. The Sonoran Desert toad, *Bufo alvarius,* formerly called the Colorado River toad, has been popularized by songs and stories about "toad-licking." It is native to and found only in the southwestern United States and Mexico.

Spadefoot toads are also anurans, but they are not in the true toad family of Bufonidae. None of the spadefoots are poisonous. They get their name from the keratinous bone on their hind feet that forms a metatarsal "spade" used for burrowing backwards in wet soil. They can be easily distinguished from true toads by their vertical pupils and the absence of parotoid glands.

Sonoran Desert Toad (*Bufo alvarius*)
POISONOUS

Range and habitat Of the 200 species of *Bufo* toads, only *Bufo alvarius* exists exclusively within the Sonoran Desert (the southern half of Arizona, southwest corner of New Mexico, southeastern California, and south into Sonora,

Mexico). They are semi-aquatic, living from sea level to elevations of about 5,300 feet (1,600 m) in arid and semi-arid habitats. They prefer grassland or brushy desert, especially creosote and mesquite, near a lake, stream, spring, watering hole, pond, or other permanent source of water; occasionally they are found near temporary water sources such as drainage ditches or rain pools.

Diet Carnivorous, Sonoran Desert toads will eat nearly anything moving that they can swallow, including snails, spiders, grasshoppers, lizards, mice, and smaller toads; their long, sticky tongues are used to catch and pull in prey. A 6-inch-long Sonoran Desert toad can eat several 3½-inch-long hard-shelled palo verde root borer beetles—an absolutely unbelievable sight!

Life span 12–25 years.

Physical characteristics The Sonoran Desert toad is the largest native toad in the United States, with a length of about 3 to 7 inches (7.5–18 cm) and a weight up to two pounds (900 g). As with most amphibians, the females are usually larger than the males. The body is stout, with a broad, flat head and short legs. The color is olive to dark brown, and the leathery skin appears relatively smooth and shiny. As with other true toads of the family Bufonidae, the pupils are horizontal. There are one or two white raised bumps at each corner of the mouth. The belly is cream-colored and usually unmarked. The very large, poison-producing, elongated, and raised parotoid glands (not "parotid" glands) originate on either side of the head behind the eyes and above the tympanums (ears), and touch the prominent cranial crests while extending downward toward the end of the neck. There are large warty-appearing glands on the hind legs called femorals, and another pair on the distal legs called tibials. Each of these glands contains small lobules that connect into ducts that join to form a single pore on the surface of the skin. All of the glands are capable of secreting the milky-white *Bufo* poison.

Behavior The Sonoran Desert toad is strongly nocturnal and spends daylight hours within rodent burrows or in other hidden, protected areas underground and out of the desert heat. In the evening, especially after heavy monsoon rains, the otherwise solitary toads emerge and congregate in wet areas near sources of water. They sometimes appear after the summer rains have arrived, but before seasonal pools fill during the breeding season of May through July. In general, the Sonoran Desert toad is more aquatic than most other toads, at times even taking up residence in a back yard swimming pool! These toads hibernate underground during the winter and do not emerge after winter rains.

Fluid balance in the toad is maintained by a very important, specific area of the belly skin (called the "seat patch") that is used for absorbing water. This patch of skin is responsible for over 70 percent of the water uptake in a dehydrated toad. A dehydrated toad will press its belly skin onto a moist surface to absorb water. If it senses that the concentration of salt in the water is too high, it will try to avoid contact with that surface and will seek out a location with a lower salt content.

A Sonoran Desert toad that has been molested or otherwise threatened will secrete a thick, milky-white poison from its glands. This poison will irritate mucous membranes and can cause cardiac and neurologic disorders and is thus a good deterrent towards coyotes and other large predators. Dogs, for some reason, seem to have a pathological passion for "playing" with these toads, and they frequently fall victim to the poison they ingest while licking or picking up the toads by mouth.

Reproduction The breeding season starts after the summer rains arrive. Males croak incessantly, giving off a low-pitched toot that lasts less than a second. Although their call is relatively weak, it is thought to attract females. The Sonoran Desert toad breeds in temporary pools formed from rain or runoff. Often, many males will attempt to mate with the same female, resulting in a large mass of toads clinging to a single female. Ultimately, only a single male from the group will succeed in mating with the female, in a process called *amplexus,* whereby the male grasps the female while she is laying eggs and fertilizes the eggs with a fluid stream containing sperm. The eggs, known as toadspawn, will hatch into tadpoles after about a month. The yellow-brown tadpoles will develop into toadlets, and eventually into toads. They must grow to a length of about 3 inches before they become sexually mature.

Effects of poison The Arizona Drug and Poison Information Center has no reports of human deaths from Sonoran Desert toad poisoning, but about 40–50 dogs die every year from ingesting or even just mouthing this toad, a clear testament to the potency of the poison.

The milky secretions from the glands of the Sonoran Desert toad contain over 26 biologically active compounds, including potent cardiovascular toxins known as *bufodienolides* and another substance called 5-MeO-DMT, which produces psychoactive effects. The cardiotoxic bufodienolides, including bufogenin and bufotoxin, are structurally similar to the cardiac drug called digitalis that is purified from the foxglove plant. The bufodienolides are well-absorbed in the gut, and ingesting crude toad poison (and even topical exposure from carelessly handling toads) may result in severe headache, nausea and violent vomiting, irregular heart rhythms, blurred vision, and seizures. Severe toxic reactions, including death, have occurred after mouthing the closely related cane toad, *Bufo marinus,* and following ingestion of an entire cane toad, toad soup, or toad eggs. Unlike digitalis and other cardiac glycosides found in plants, the bufodienolides lack an attached sugar molecule that prevents many substances from crossing the blood-brain barrier; this allows the bufodienolides to more easily pass into the brain and induce seizures. There are many reports of seizures after ingestion of toad poison, but few after ingestion of digitalis or the foxglove plant.

The presence of the potent hallucinogen 5-MeO-DMT in the secretions of *Bufo alvarius* has led many people to ingest the poison in an attempt to experience the psychoactive and/or psychedelic effects. Rather than the expected hallucinations, the usual result is a severe poisoning comparable to a digitalis overdose. The cardiotoxic bufodienolides in the toad secretions are well-absorbed in the gut, whereas the hallucinogenic 5-MeO-DMT is inactivated in the gut by monoamine oxidase (unless the person is taking a drug called a monoamine oxidase inhibitor!) and never makes it into the circulation or to the brain. Ingestions of the poisonous secretions are therefore dominated by the profound effects of the cardiotoxic compounds, leading to nausea, violent vomiting, severe headache, and potentially low blood pressure and death by cardiovascular collapse. Because 5-MeO-DMT is inactivated in the gut, there is virtually no possibility of having a "psychedelic" experience by ingesting the secretions, which explains why toad licking is not a very popular recreational means of getting "high."

Interestingly, the hallucinogenic compound 5-MeO-DMT is heat-stable, whereas the cardiotoxic bufodienolides are not. The integrative medicine physician Dr. Andrew Weil reported that the crude poison from *Bufo alvarius* can be collected, dried, and smoked. The bufodienolides are inactivated by the heat, and the 5-MeO-DMT remains pharmacologically active. Along with Weil's other ethnopharmacological research, the fact that the tryptamine derivative 5-MeO-DMT is found only in *Bufo alvarius* and not in other toads led to the hypothesis that the pre-Columbian peoples of the New World may have smoked the dried secretions from this toad as a ritual intoxicant.

The amount of this substance in Sonoran Desert poison is rather high. One *Bufo alvarius* may yield 0.5 gram of crude poison, containing 75 mg of 5-MeO-DMT; the effective (hallucinogenic) dose in humans is 3–5 mg.

FIRST AID AND MEDICAL TREATMENT It is important to remember to wash your hands soon after handling a Sonoran Desert toad, particularly before touching your eyes or mouth. If a dog has been mouthing a Sonoran Desert toad, wash its mouth out quickly and firmly with water from a garden hose, controlling the flow of water so that it washes sideways and not down the dog's throat, and seek veterinary assistance immediately.

Accidental poisonings from the Sonoran Desert toad are uncommon in humans, and most victims have intentionally ingested the toxic toad secretions. First aid for *Bufo alvarius* poisoning involves safely transporting the victim to a hospital for further supportive care, preferably by ambulance. The primary concerns are treating the symptoms of nausea and vomiting, as well as managing the potential cardiovascular effects of the poison and any seizure activity. The bufodienolides in the poison may cause a high blood-potassium level and cardiac arrhythmias or even cardiac arrest; these have been treated successfully with DigiBind, the antidote for digitalis toxicity. Seizures may also respond to DigiBind or to Dilantin.

There is no specific treatment available for the hallucinogenic effects of 5-MeO-DMT, and someone who is experiencing severe psychotropic effects from inhaled, smoked toad secretions may require sedation until the 5-MeO-DMT has been completely metabolized and the effects have worn off.

Ingesting or smoking *Bufo alvarius* secretions certainly falls in the category called "Don't try this at home," or for that matter, anywhere else!

Red Spotted Toad (*Bufo punctatus*)
NON-POISONOUS

Range and habitat Red spotted toads are found from southern Nevada to southwestern Kansas, south into north

ern Mexico and throughout Baja California; they are commonly found in rocky streams and arroyos, and sometimes on manmade waterfalls and in swimming pools.

Diet They eat insects and other arthropods.

Life span Several years.

Physical characteristics The red spotted toad is a true toad that is easily identified by its flattened appearance, small size (1.5–3 inches, or 3.7–7.5 cm), and the red or orange warts for which it is named. The underlying color is dark green or olive. Unlike other toads, the red spotted toad has *round* parotoid glands that are about the same size as the eyes. As with all true toads, the pupils are horizontal. Unlike the Sonoran Desert toad, this toad has almost no skin secretions and is not considered poisonous.

Behavior On summer nights, red spotted toads like to sing from rocks near the edges of water, and they can sometimes be found singing from the decorative rock waterfalls of swimming pools. Their song is a high-pitched musical trill.

Reproduction This is the only toad species native to the Southwest that lays isolated, single eggs, rather than clusters of eggs. The tadpoles metamorphose in six to eight weeks.

Couch's Spadefoot (*Scaphiopus couchi*)
NON-POISONOUS

Range and habitat Their range stretches from Baja California (Mexico), southern Arizona, New Mexico, Texas, and parts of Oklahoma; habitat includes desert areas, grasslands, and areas with creosote and mesquite.

Diet Beetles, grasshoppers, katydids, crickets, and other insects and arthropods make up the diet of Couch's spadefoots.

Life span Several years.

Physical characteristics Spadefoots are not members of the true toad family, Bufonidae, but instead occupy their own family called Scaphiopodidae. They can be easily distinguished from true toads by their vertical pupils, a lack of parotoid glands, teeth in the upper jaw, and the black sickle-shaped spade on each of their hind feet. They range in size up to 3½ inches (9 cm), and have irregular blotches of dark green, brown, and black on the back.

Behavior The lamb-like bleating sound of Couch's spadefoot is a familiar chorus in the Southwest during the heavy rains of summer. Before the ground dries out in the heat of summer, spadefoots bury themselves up to 3 feet (about a meter) underground, burrowing backwards, where they will remain for ten months or more. Development is very rapid in spadefoots; egg hatching to metamorphosed toads takes less than two weeks. The skin secretions of the spadefoot do not contain toxins such as those of the Sonoran Desert toad, although the secretions may irritate the skin of some people.

Reproduction During the summer monsoon season, after the spadefoots emerge from underground, males call females to mate. During amplexus, or mating, one female can lay up to 3,000 eggs. The eggs hatch quickly into tadpoles before the shallow pools disappear, in as little as 15 hours.

Reptiles

Reptiles make up a group of about 8,000 species of cold-blooded vertebrates that are divided into four orders: the Crocodilia (crocodiles and alligators), the Rhynchocephalia (tuataras of New Zealand), the Squamata (lizards and snakes), and the Chelonia (turtles). Like birds and mammals, but unlike amphibians, reptiles are amniotes; during development, the embryo is enclosed in an amnion, a tough, membranous sac filled with fluid. Most reptiles are *oviparous* and lay eggs, although some are *ovoviviparous* and retain the eggs internally until after they hatch. Most reptiles have three-chambered hearts, a pair of lungs, and a pair of kidneys. Medical scientists have become interested in the unique metabolism of many reptiles that allows them to survive under harsh environmental conditions. One payoff for this interest in the Gila monster, in particular, was the development of a new drug for treating diabetes.

LIZARDS

Lizards are classified in a suborder of Squamata called the Sauria (or Lacertilia). Most lizards are four-legged and have both external ear openings and eyelids. (Glass lizards have no true legs, but they do have ears and eyelids.) Lizards generally have dry skin and tend not to live in water. Many lizards can change color at times of stress or to blend in with their environments; many can also regenerate lost limbs or their tails. The largest lizards in the world are monitors, such as the komodo dragon of Asia. At 175–310 lbs (80–140 kg), it is very dangerous, but non-venomous. The only venomous lizards in the world are the Gila monster and the beaded lizard of Mexico.

LEFT: Gila monster (*Heloderma suspectum*).

Gila Monster (*Heloderma suspectum*)
VENOMOUS

Range and habitat Gila monsters are indigenous to the southwest U.S. and northern Mexico, including Arizona, Utah, Nevada, New Mexico, and a small part of California; *Heloderma suspectum suspectum* (reticulated Gila monster) is found primarily in the Sonoran and Chihuahuan Deserts (adults of this species are mottled and blotched); *Heloderma suspectum cinctum* (banded Gila monster) lives primarily in the Mojave Desert (adults have a broad double-crossband across the back); other members of the genus are found farther south into Mexico. Typical habitat includes rocky desert scrub areas and mountain foothills at elevations up to 4,900 feet (1,500 meters). They are rarely found in flat agricultural areas and prefer habitat that is wet enough for shrubs; they prefer palo verde–saguaro desert scrub over the drier, sandier creosote bush–bursage habitat. These large lizards often lie and soak in shallow pools. They actively seek out burrows left by other animals or dig burrows of their own.

Diet Gila monsters eat small mammals, birds, eggs, lizards, frogs, insects, and carrion; during April and May, their diet consists mostly of eggs and young from Gambel's quail and desert cottontail nests; they may also consume the young from other small vertebrate nests.

Life span Approximately 20–30 years.

Physical characteristics The Gila monster, the only venomous lizard found in the United States, is a solitary, large, stocky-appearing lizard that grows to about 18 to 24 inches (46–60 cm) in length, with a weight of up to three to five pounds (1.4–2.3 kg). The skin is covered with small, bead-like scales that extend from the top of the head to the tail. The bead-like appearance is the result of small bones called *osteoderms* under the scales. The underbelly is covered with flat plate-like scales. The face is always black, and the rest of the skin color consists of black, orange, pink, or yellow spots, patches, and bars, in irregular patterns. Bands of color also extend across the length of the tail. The massive head is dominated by powerful jaws. The tail appears quite heavy and is used for storing fat. The only other venomous

Protection for Gila monster

Gila monsters are protected throughout their range in the U.S. and Mexico. All states in the U.S. where Gila monsters are found have regulations requiring permits for all activities involving these animals. International trade in Gila monsters is regulated by the Convention on International Trade in Endangered Species. Gila monsters are not now considered threatened with extinction, but could become threatened unless their trade is strictly regulated.

lizard in the world is the predominantly black beaded lizard, *Heloderma horridum,* found only in Mexico. It lacks the orange, pink, or yellow coloration of the Gila monster.

Behavior The Gila monster spends the majority of its life underground, virtually inactive. Gila monsters have reasonably good claws and can be persistent diggers, and they will hide as well as hibernate in burrows or under rocks. In spring and early summer, when food is more available, Gila monsters may be observed foraging for quail or rodent nests. Although often thought of as nocturnal animals, they are primarily diurnal and are most often seen in the early morning or late afternoon and early evening. This is particularly true during the summer rainy season, when they are most active and intent on feeding and finding mates.

Gila monsters hunt by primarily using their sense of taste and smell, rather than eyesight. By flicking the tongue in the air and against objects, they pick up scent molecules on the tongue and deposit them in the roof of the mouth on a structure called "Jacobson's organ," a trait they share with snakes.

A Gila monster can consume a large amount of food in a single feeding—up to a third of its body weight for adults and 50 percent of its body weight for young Gilas. An adult male can consume its entire yearly energy budget in three or four meals. Given their very low metabolic rate, this "binge-eating" allows them to store calories in their abdomens and tails as fat, for use during times when food is scarce and during the roughly four months they spend in hibernation (November–February). Immediately after they eat, large amounts of a hormone called *extendin* are released into the blood. The extendin, in turn, causes the prolonged release of insulin, which prevents the blood sugar from rising and converts the animal's metabolism to conserve the consumed calories as fat. A synthetic version of extendin called *exenatide* was recently developed as a treatment for diabetes in humans and is being sold under the trade name Byetta. Gila monsters are also poikilothermic (cold-blooded), and their metabolism becomes extremely slow when the ambient temperature drops, as well as during hibernation.

Gila monsters appear sluggish and slow compared with other lizards. They are often seen ambling slowly yet deliberately, using flicks of their forked tongues against the ground to sense their environment. When accosted, they often attempt to avoid interaction by changing direction. If threatened, they freeze and hiss loudly, with the mouth open, revealing the size of the massive jaws. When approached from behind, they have an uncanny ability to turn 180 degrees in a split second, surprising and biting the aggressor with powerful jaws and razor-sharp teeth. Unlike venomous snakes that will bite, envenomate, and release, Gila monsters hang on tenaciously while gnawing with their teeth, allowing venom from the glands in their lower jaws to flow into the wound.

Reproduction Gila monsters court and mate between April and June. Copulation lasts approximately an hour. Roughly 42–55 days after mating, females lay 3–15 leathery eggs in sandy soil, about 5 inches (13 cm) deep, which allows the sun to heat the sand and incubate the eggs. The eggs develop over winter and hatch in the spring. Interestingly, there is no other lizard in North America that lays eggs that over-winter and hatch the following year. The brightly colored newborns are about 3½–4½ inches (9–11 cm) long and will require one to three years to reach adult size.

Effects of venom The venom of Gila monsters is complex and similar to that of the elapid group of venomous snakes, such as coral snakes. Unlike venomous snakes, however, Gila monsters have venom glands in their lower jaws, rather than in the upper jaws. The venom glands are modified salivary glands, and they produce more than 20 different toxins that can act synergistically. Gila monsters do not have fangs, but instead have grooved teeth that are used to direct the venom into the wound by capillary action. They typically bite for a prolonged time, to allow the penetration of a sufficient amount of venom. The venom itself primarily contains neurotoxins and causes respiratory failure in prey, although it usually causes only extreme pain in humans, as well as swelling, nausea, vomiting, and occasionally bleeding. Rarely, fatalities have occurred, as has anaphylaxis to the proteins contained in the venom. The primary toxins in Gila monster venom are called gilatoxin, hemorrhagic toxin, and phospholipase A2. There is also a component called hyaluronidase that causes tissue breakdown and aids in the spread of venom away from the area that was bitten. You don't want to experience this bite!

FIRST AID AND MEDICAL TREATMENT The first priority should be to firmly hold and carefully remove the biting Gila monster as quickly as possible. This is best accomplished by prying the jaws off with a stick or object like a pen or screwdriver. The longer the Gila monster remains attached, the greater the amount of venom that will be absorbed.

Wash or rinse the wound immediately and keep the affected body part at the level of the heart. Immediately seek or request medical attention. Do not use a tourniquet or other constrictive dressing (unless the victim becomes unconscious), and do not use ice or cut or suck on the wound—this will likely make the injury worse.

There is no antivenom available for Gila monster bites, and the primary medical treatment is pain management and basic or advanced life support. The severe pain will likely last eight hours or more. Although there have been no confirmed deaths due solely to a Gila monster bite, a prolonged bite of 30–45 seconds potentially could be fatal to an adult or a child. There have been cases of severe envenomation resulting in very low blood pressure, airway swelling, and heart damage, so urgent medical evaluation is mandatory.

The best way to avoid getting bitten is to avoid physical contact with a Gila monster, as they will not bite unless approached or provoked. There is simply no justification for being envenomated by one of these beautiful and uncommon desert dwellers. Enjoy watching this spectacularly colored lizard from at least 5 feet (1.5 m) away and you will take home a most memorable experience.

Banded Gecko (*Coleonyx variegatus*)
NON-VENOMOUS

Range and habitat Banded geckos are found across the Southwest, particularly in the Sonoran and Mojave Deserts; they favor arid areas and desert grasslands, canyons, hillsides, and areas providing rocks or other shelter. They are also found in sandy arroyos and dunes—and are also often found in garages.

Diet They dine on insects and other arthropods.

Life span Geckos may live many years.

Physical characteristics The banded gecko is often erroneously thought to be venomous or to have poisonous skin, or it is mistaken for a baby Gila monster because of the similarity in pattern when viewed from above. Unlike Gila monsters, geckos are not beaded, and they only grow to a

maximum length of 6 inches (15 cm), about half of which is tail. They have large, protruding eyes and functional eyelids that are lined with white (most geckos, like all snakes, cannot close their eyes). Geckos are unique among the lizards for their ability to communicate with each other by chirping or squealing.

Behavior The tail is used as an energy store for fat, particularly for winter or other times when food is scarce. If a gecko is caught by the tail, the tail can break off to allow escape, although this may leave the gecko without sufficient fat stores for the winter. The tail regrows quickly, but the replacement tail cannot be released and often does not have the same pattern as the original. Geckos are strongly nocturnal and can wave their tails in a scorpion-like manner to discourage predators.

Reproduction Two eggs are laid in late spring; females can lay two clutches a year. After six weeks, the eggs hatch into 1-inch-long (2.5 cm) baby geckos.

Horned Lizard (*Phrynosoma* species)
NON-VENOMOUS

Range and habitat Of the 13 species of horned lizards, five inhabit the deserts of the American Southwest and in particular the Sonoran Desert region (southwestern Arizona, extreme southeastern California, a small part of northeastern Baja California, Mexico, and the upper neck of north-

western Sonora, Mexico); others are found as far south as Guatemala and as far north as southern Canada. Habitats include hills and rocky mountain areas, fine sand, and short grasslands.

Diet Horned lizards eat ants and other insects, and occasionally other invertebrates.

Life span Horned lizards can live for several years.

Physical characteristics With squat, flat, toad-like bodies and thorn-like projections at the rear of their heads, horned lizards are easily distinguished from other lizards. Often incorrectly called "horny toads" or "horned toads," these prehistoric-looking lizards depend on camouflage and a fierce appearance for survival, rather than speed or venom. Horned lizards have snout-to-vent lengths of up to 2½–5 inches (6–12 cm) and an overall length of up to about 8 inches (20 cm).

Behavior If handled, a horned lizard will often turn its head to try to stick one of the horns into a finger—but this seldom breaks the skin. When frightened, horned lizards can increase the pressure within the capillaries of one of their eyes until the blood vessels break and blood shoots out. This distraction often results in their escape.

Reproduction The female lays eggs between May and August, with clutches ranging from 3 to 45, depending on

the species. Generally only a couple from each clutch will survive to reach sexual maturity. The short-horned lizard (*Phrynosoma douglassii*) of the northern U.S. and Canada bears live young, which is generally considered an adaptation to higher latitudes, where eggs are subject to lower temperatures.

SNAKES

The Serpentes, or snakes, are a suborder of the order Squamata (lizards and snakes). There are five taxonomic families of snakes in the United States, and knowing which family a snake belongs to quickly tells you a lot about it. The Boidae are all constrictors, like the boas; the Colubridae or colubrids are common snakes like the garter snake; the Leptotyphlopidae are the small, slender blind snakes; the Elapidae or elapids are best known internationally as cobras, kraits, and mambas—in North America, they're represented by the coral snakes; and the Viperidae or vipers are represented in America by the pit vipers, including rattlesnakes, copperheads, and cottonmouths.

Most snakes in the United States are non-venomous colubrids. The only dangerously venomous snakes here are the elapids and the vipers. The front-fanged and neurotoxic elapids are represented in the Southwest by the small, weakly venomous Sonoran or Western coral snake (*Micruroides euryxanthus*), which is seldom actually encountered and is rarely responsible for significant envenomations. Its cousin, the dangerous Eastern coral snake (*Micrurus fulvius*), is found in the Southeast but not in the Southwest. By far the most common venomous snakes in the western U.S. are the front-fanged pit vipers (the Crotalinae or crotalines), represented by about 15 species of rattlesnake in two genera (*Crotalus* and *Sistrurus*). Rattlesnakes are responsible for the vast majority of venomous snakebites in the Southwest. The rattle-less copperheads and cottonmouths (both of the genus *Agkistrodon*) resemble rattlesnakes in many ways, including many components of their venom, but they are not found further west than central Texas.

Rattlesnakes (*Crotalus* and *Sistrurus* species)
VENOMOUS

Range and habitat Although rattlesnakes are found across most of the U.S., the greatest diversity of species and highest overall density are in the Southwest. Preferred areas range from lowlands of the deserts to elevations above 7,000 feet (2,134 m); the species most likely to be encountered depends on geographic location, elevation, and particular habitat. Habitats can range from deep woods to rocky outcroppings to sand dunes.

Diet Rattlesnakes eat small rodents such as ground squirrels, mice, rats, and baby rabbits; birds; arthropods such as the giant desert centipede; lizards, toads, frogs, and even other snakes. They will also eat bird and reptile eggs; their primary requirement is that prey must be swallowed whole, as rattlesnakes are unable to chew.

Life span Up to 20 years in captivity.

Physical characteristics Size and color pattern are helpful in identifying rattlesnakes, but these characteristics alone are seldom adequate for making an accurate identification.

Western diamondback rattlesnake (*Crotalus atrox*).

Many rattlesnakes have similar appearances, and many non-venomous snakes are easily confused with rattlesnakes. While "size does matter," accurately estimating the length of living rattlesnakes is not easy, as can be shown by comparison of the estimates of length with actual measurements of newly deceased snakes. Estimates of length are compli-cated by the fact that rattlesnakes are usually found coiled up and not stretched out, and they are often less-than-cooperative in assuming a stretched-out position.

The average overall size and length vary greatly and depend on the species. Our smallest rattlesnake, the pigmy rattlesnake (*Sistrurus miliarius streckeri*), reaches a length of less than 2 feet (38–56 cm), while the largest rattler in the

United States, the Eastern diamondback (*Crotalus adamanteus*), may measure up to 8 feet in length (244 cm). The Western diamondback is the largest rattlesnake in the Southwest and is only slightly smaller than its Eastern cousin, with maximum lengths of up to 7 feet (213 cm). Newborn rattlesnakes are surprisingly large, with average lengths of about 7 inches (18 cm) for the smaller species to about 13 inches (33 cm) for newborn Western diamondbacks.

The most notable characteristic of all rattlesnakes found in the United States is the presence of the rattle (or rattle string) at the end of the tail. The lightweight, hollow rattle string is composed of interlocking rattle segments with multiple lobes on each segment. Lateral, or sideways, vibra-

Color-marking a rattle for field identification.

tion of the tail along with a slight twisting motion results in the characteristic high-pitched buzzing or hissing sound. It is impossible to reproduce this sound by shaking a rattle in the hand, as human muscle is no match for the high-frequency vibration of 25–100 cycles per second produced by the rattlesnake's specialized tail muscles. The frequency of vibration depends on the snake's temperament or level of agitation, the body temperature and the size. The warmer the snake or the more agitated it is, the faster the rattle. Everything else being equal, the bigger the snake, the slower the frequency of the rattle.

The function of the rattle has been debated for centuries, but it is now clearly thought to serve as a warning to anything that might potentially harm the snake. Rattlesnakes in the wild are seldom observed using their rattles unless they have been disturbed, and they do not use their rattles to distract or attract prey (such as inquisitive birds), or to locate other rattlesnakes.

The size of the rattle and its relationship to the rattlesnake's age is often a source of controversy. Many myths abound, including the myth that rattlesnakes have no rattle at all for up to three years, or that they "throw off" their rattles (they don't, although they can break off), or that they have enormous rattles with up to 50 segments. In truth, wild rattlesnakes usually have fewer than 16 rattle segments, although snakes raised in captivity may have more. Another misconception is that all species of rattlesnakes can rattle—the Santa Catalina Island rattlesnake has only a single-segment rattle that can't make noise.

Tiger rattlesnake (*Crotalus tigris*).

Baby rattlesnakes are also not able to rattle, although they can certainly strike and envenomate! They are born with nothing more than a pre-button on the tail, which is shed a few days after birth, revealing the button, the first permanent part of the rattle. Successive sheddings add new segments to the rattle; thus rattlesnakes are able to rattle after they have shed at least twice and have both a rattle segment and a button. If a rattle is complete and unbroken, the relatively smooth button is always the very last segment on the tail; otherwise, the somewhat sharp lobes of a terminal rattle are visible.

The segments of the rattle string are counted starting from the button (called "rattle number one") towards the head of the snake (number 2, number 3, etc.). Shedding may take place several times in one season, and therefore simply counting the number of segments (even if none are broken off) is unlikely to give an accurate age of a rattlesnake. If the rattle string is broken and the button is missing, it is impossible to accurately count the number of segments.

The color and pattern of rattlesnakes is highly variable, even within a single species. The colors range from black to muted shades of browns, oranges, yellows, greens, and reds. Blues are uncommon and are perhaps revealed only in the lavender-phase tiger rattlesnake (*C. tigris*). The yellows can appear as brilliant as sparkling gold in some black-tailed (*C. molossus*), Southern Pacific (*C. viridis helleri*), and Arizona black (*C. viridis cerberus*) rattlers. Color can vary so much that even two snakes of the same species may not even appear related. For example, some Mojave rattlesnakes (*C. scutulatus*) look dark brown, while others appear to be a bright olive green. In addition, aberrant color variations are known to exist, such as albino (amelanistic) and hypomelanistic (having less black pigment and therefore more brightly colored than normal) snakes, as well as rattlesnakes lacking any

Southern Pacific rattlesnake (*Crotalus viridis helleri*).

pattern or having a bizarre pattern such as zigzagging or striping. Rarely, rattlesnakes have been found that have piebaldism, a strange affliction that results in large, irregularly located patches of white.

The most predominant pattern in rattlesnakes is a repeating series of dark hexagons surrounded by light-colored scales that run down the back of the snake, often morphing into a nondescript pattern near the tail. The overall pattern is by no means universal, and some rattlesnakes have an almost square pattern on the back, such as the prairie rattler (*C. viridis viridis*), or a diffuse banding such as the speckled rattlesnake (*C. mitchellii*) or the mottled rock rattlesnake (*C. lepidus*). Rattlesnake tails are often banded or barred, in either black and white or dark and light, but this is also not absolute.

While the rattle may get your attention, the "business end" of the rattlesnake is obviously the head. The rattlesnake head possesses three of the defining characteristics of pit vipers: the hinged, hollow front teeth, or fangs; eyes with vertical pupils; and a heat-sensing *loreal pit* located on each side of the head between the nostril and the upper jaw. The scale pattern on the head is also one of the most reliable methods of identifying a particular species of rattlesnake, although getting close enough to see the scale pattern on a live, unrestrained rattlesnake is not recommended! Unlike other families of snakes such as the colubrids and the elapids, the rattlesnake head is triangular, more so in *Crotalus* species than in *Sistrurus*. This often gives rattlesnakes the appearance of having wide cheek-

Arizona black rattlesnake (*Crotalus viridus cerberus*).

bones, which can be a useful aid for quick identification of a non-rattling snake.

A rattlesnake's fangs function like hypodermic needles to deliver venom. These long, thin, hollow specialized front teeth fold up and lie flat against the roof of the mouth when not in use. Within the gum, the base of each fang is connected to the venom apparatus that lies further back in the mouth. Fangs are frequently broken off or shed, and new fangs replace the lost ones within a few weeks. The fangs are extended to about 90 degrees only to inject venom; otherwise, they are retracted and are not used when swallowing prey.

Who gets bitten?

Rattlesnake bites result in significant injury and disability and have the potential to kill—therefore, the prevention of snakebite is important. Fortunately, most rattlesnake bites can be prevented. Snakebites are classified into two categories based on the circumstances of the bite. "Legitimate" bites are those where the recipient was not intentionally interacting with the snake. This is contrasted with "illegitimate" bites, where the recipient was intentionally interacting with and often provoking the snake. Illegitimate bites are obviously preventable. If you don't want to get bitten, stay back and don't mess with a rattlesnake!

About three-fourths of all rattlesnake bites in the Southwest occur between April and September, when both snakes and people are more active outdoors. Statistically, males are bitten by rattlesnakes two to four times more often than females. One recent study of rattlesnake bites showed that the average victim was 24 years old, three out of five victims were intentionally handling the snake, about a quarter of all bite victims appeared to be intoxicated, and four out of five were bitten on the finger(s) or hand. Another study of several hundred snakebite victims in Arizona found that 85 percent were

males and about one in five bites occurred in children less than 13 years of age. The message is clear—if you don't intentionally interact with a rattlesnake, the odds of getting bitten are pretty low!

The risk of getting bitten by a rattlesnake can be reduced by following some simple precautions:

- If you find a venomous snake, leave it alone and don't molest it.

- Wear thick leather boots and gaiters (shin guards) when walking through tall grass, and stay on trails whenever possible.

- Avoid placing your hands or feet in places that you cannot see, particularly when scrambling on rocks or when picking up wood.

- You should also avoid handling dead snakes and decapitated snake heads. The bite reflex can persist for up to an hour in the head of a decapitated snake. Envenomations have been reported from both recently dead, decapitated snakes and even from preserved specimens.

Mojave rattlesnake (*Crotalus scutulatus*).

The loreal pit is an extremely heat-sensitive organ used by rattlesnakes to locate and "image" prey. Each pit opens into a cavity that contains a highly vascular membrane covered with a dense array of heat-sensing nerves. This heat-sensing system is analogous to an infrared imaging device and is sensitive enough for a nocturnal rattlesnake to "visualize" a mouse at 2 feet (60 cm) and deliver a precise, fatal strike and envenomation. This imaging system may also let the snake know if it has encountered something too large to be considered prey and that it should switch from offensive to defensive behavior.

The rattlesnake's tongue has no taste buds but is a very efficient collector of airborne molecules that can characterize the local environment, including the presence of prey. These molecules are trapped on the tongue and then deposited in the mouth near the Jacobsen's organ, which lies in the roof of the mouth. Jacobsen's organ is a highly sensitive chemoreceptor associated with the olfactory nerve—the same nerve that gives us our sense of smell. The use of this system enables rattlesnakes to track down their envenomated prey.

Behavior "Rattlesnake!" No other word can stop a hiker in his tracks as fast, or send such an electrifying chill up the spine. The unexpected, hissing buzz of a nearby rattler can be even more unnerving and will strike fear in the hearts of even the most experienced outdoorsman. Over 1,000 people a year are bitten by rattlesnakes. At least half of those are referred to as "illegitimate" bites and are the result of someone intentionally interacting with a snake. Most of those bitten suffer some permanent disability, but fortunately, only a handful of people a year die from rattlesnake bites. For comparison, about 15,000 people a year are stung by bees and wasps, and nationally there are about 4.7 *million* dog bites a year, resulting in about 20 deaths. Still, even though the overall risk of getting bitten by a rattlesnake is very low, the consequences can be severe.

As *poikilothermic,* or cold-blooded, animals, rattlesnakes depend on their surroundings for heat. This dictates much of their behavior. During the cold winter months, rattlesnakes avoid potentially deadly freezing temperatures by hibernating in dens called *hibernacula.* As temperatures warm up, they leave the hibernacula in search of food, water, and warmth, and are more likely to cross paths with people.

Somewhat surprisingly, rattlesnakes are more tolerant of low temperatures than of heat. A few minutes at temperatures of 110 degrees F (43 degrees C) can kill a rattlesnake. Given that their prey also tends to avoid heat, rattlesnakes are encountered far more often at night or in the mornings and evenings, rather than during the middle of the day (especially during the summer), when they typically seek shelter. If daytime temperatures are low, you may come across rattlesnakes sunning themselves to increase their body temperatures.

Shedding, or molting, is a necessary component of snake growth and occurs anywhere from one to six times a year. Younger snakes and those in warmer habitats shed more frequently than older snakes or those in cool climates. About seven to ten days before shedding, fluid accumulates under the old skin and the snake's eyes develop a blue cast. The snake's vision is decreased and it will frequently find a safe place to hide until shedding is complete. The head is the first place where the old skin begins to peel off, often as a result of the snake rubbing its jaw or head against a rough rock. As the skin begins to peel back, the snake finds a tight fit somewhere between rocks or branches to snag the skin and allow it to proceed forward, leaving the old skin turned inside-out. The color and patterns of the new skin are bright and vivid, and will diminish with time and aging until the snake undergoes yet another shed.

Rattlesnakes seldom track down or pursue their intended prey. Instead, they pick an area frequented by prey and then lie in wait for it. Mice and other rodents frequently run along walls and fences, which explains why rattlesnakes are often encountered in similar locations. When prey comes within range, a lightning-fast strike envenomates it, then rapid tongue-flicks are used to carefully track the prey to the location of its demise. Further tongue-flicks are used to locate the head of the victim, allowing it to be consumed head first.

Southwestern speckled rattlesnake (*Crotalus mitchellii*).

Rattlesnakes can climb trees and are sometimes found in low-growing shrubs or tree branches. For the most part, however, rattlesnakes are not arboreal. Rattlesnakes can also swim, though they are seldom found in water.

If threatened, rattlesnakes quickly assume the well-known defensive posture, with the body coiled, the head raised up in an S-shaped loop, and the tail elevated and rattling. This posture is seen only when rattlesnakes have been disturbed or otherwise threatened. It is not used when the snakes are hunting or during courtship. Rattlesnakes generally prefer not to interact with non-prey. Given the opportunity, they will flee into cover rather than take on an aggressor. They also don't always rattle before striking in defense, as anyone who has been bitten while walking in tall grass or reaching onto a ledge or overhang will testify.

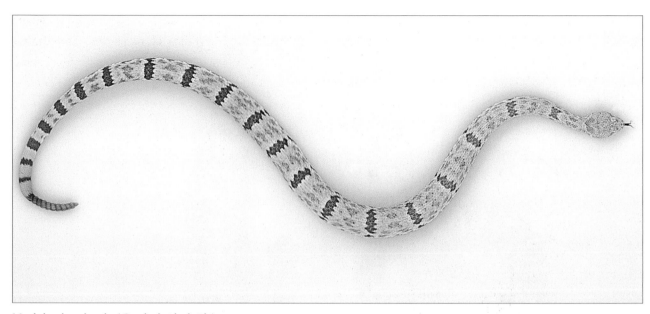

Mottled rock rattlesnake (*Crotalus lepidus lepidus*).

There is often confusion regarding the terms "bite" and "strike." To bite, a rattlesnake must only open its mouth and embed its fangs. A restrained rattlesnake can bite (as can a decapitated rattlesnake head), but it can't strike, which involves coordinated movement of the head, neck, and body of the snake.

Unrestrained rattlesnakes typically deliver a bite via a "strike," the rapid movement of the head towards a target, carried out by extension of the head and front (anterior) part of the body, with the middle and tail end (posterior) of the body remaining stationary. While a rattlesnake can *bite* from a fully extended or uncoiled body position, strikes are generally delivered from a "striking coil"—an open anchor loop, elevated forebody, and an "S"-shaped bend in the neck. The strike generally consists of four phases: preparation, launch, the bite (which includes fang penetration and envenomation), and recoil. The strike is so fast that the rattlesnake head cannot be followed by the human eye. Strike speeds measured at mid-strike in the prairie rattlesnake averaged 8 feet per second. The total duration of a strike, measured from launch, is usually less than half a second. Rattlesnakes can strike a distance of approximately half their body length.

Strikes can be classified as either defensive or predatory. In both, a premium is placed on an accurate strike that produces ideal fang placement and good envenomation. Prey is rapidly released after a bite prior to "recoil," presumably to minimize the risk of injury to the snake. Venom is not always released in a bite (or a strike), which gives rise to the term "dry bite," a bite without significant envenomation. Dry bites are estimated to occur in 3 to 35 percent of all defensive strikes; they seldom occur in predatory strikes.

The rattlesnake strike involves tremendous versatility and variation in the use of different body segments and postures. Control of the strike is based primarily on sensory inputs from the eyes and the heat-sensing loreal pits during the launch of the strike, and on tactile stimuli after contact. When small errors are made in targeting, rattlesnakes do not change the trajectory of the strike to make corrections. Instead, after the snake makes contact with the target, the fangs are repositioned. To reduce the impact force on the snake's jaws and fangs, the head decelerates prior to making

Sidewinder (*Crotalus cerastes*).

contact with the target. After penetration of the fang(s) into the victim, venom is injected through one or both fangs by contraction of the muscles surrounding the venom glands. Muscular contraction increases pressure within the venom gland, forcing venom out, in a manner analogous to a syringe and hypodermic needle. After envenomation, having accomplished their mission, the fangs are quickly withdrawn from the victim and returned to their retracted position.

Rattlesnakes are able to control, or meter, the amount of venom that is delivered during a bite, depending on prey size or behavioral context. Defensive strikes have significantly longer durations of venom flow than predatory strikes and deliver approximately ten times more venom. The duration of fang penetration is almost always longer than venom flow, and backwards or retrograde venom flow or "suctioning" usually occurs on fang withdrawal. This may serve to keep excess venom out of the fang, where it could crystallize and create a blockage. If one fang does not penetrate the prey or target, venom generally does not flow out of it; the fang is re-positioned and a second pulse of venom flow occurs.

Reproduction Courtship between male and female rattlesnakes may take place during the spring, summer, or fall, depending on the species. A well-nourished, mature and healthy female rattlesnake will release pheromones after shedding that serve as a stimulant to male snakes, which in turn may track the scent for miles. Male rattlesnakes that encounter other males during this period will engage in ritualistic "combat," with both snakes rising up tall, intertwining their necks, and using their bodies to try to push down the competition. Eventually, one of the two males gives up and retreats in defeat, leaving the victor to pursue mating with the female.

Rattlesnake mating may take place over hours or even days, during which time the male and female remain side-by-side and move very little, attached at the *vent* on the underside to allow sperm transfer. The mating act may be repeated several times, after which the male and female go their separate ways. The female may store the sperm for many months prior to fertilization, allowing her to optimize the timing of gestation. After fertilization occurs, rattlesnake young begin development within the female. She will seldom eat while pregnant, and will carefully thermoregulate by changing her location. The number of young that develop is dependent on the species and size of the snake, but often falls between 10 and 20.

Rattlesnakes are viviparous, giving birth to live young rather than laying eggs as most other reptiles do. Baby rattlesnakes are usually born at night and are vigorously protected by their mothers until after their first shed, when they will venture off on their own. The mortality of newborn rattlesnakes is relatively high, as it is for many other reptiles and birds. Baby rattlesnakes can deliver a significant amount of venom during a strike, and their venom has a different composition than that of adult rattlesnakes.

Blacktail rattlesnake (*Crotalus molossus*).

Effects of venom The clinical effects of envenomation include pain, swelling, and tenderness at the bite site, swelling and bruising away from the bite site, low blood pressure and lightheadedness, nausea, vomiting, diarrhea, numbness (especially around the mouth), *fasciculations* or muscle twitching, difficulty breathing, confusion, and ultimately unconsciousness. Frequently, the limb that has been bitten and envenomated will swell tremendously and will become purple from blood that has leaked out of blood vessels. Blood blisters may also form, especially on the fingers or toes.

The complications from rattlesnake bites include local tissue and skin breakdown (including the need for skin grafts), muscle breakdown (called *rhabdomyolysis*), amputation, chronic arthritis, limb weakness and decreased joint mobility, systemic neurotoxicity that can paralyze the mus-

Banded rock rattlesnake (*Crotalus lepidus klauberi*).

cles used for breathing, stroke, kidney failure, blood-clotting disorders and internal bleeding, miscarriage, fluid in the lungs (pulmonary edema or pulmonary hemorrhage), circulatory collapse from the leakage of fluid out of the vascular system, and *anaphylaxis* (a severe allergic reaction that can include loss of airway due to swelling as well as cardiovascular collapse). Fortunately, knowing something about rattlesnakes can help prevent your becoming a statistic.

Rattlesnakes and other crotalids use their venom primarily to immobilize, kill, and digest prey, and as a defense against predators and aggressors. The primary mechanism of venom toxicity is a massive leakage of blood vessels, causing cardiovascular shock from a loss of fluid from the vascular system into the surrounding tissues. In addition, the venom interferes with the normal blood clotting mechanism, thereby increasing the rate of internal bleeding. The components of some crotaline venoms, especially Mojave toxin, also cause neuromuscular paralysis, which can result in death from respiratory arrest. The combination is an impressively toxic cocktail!

Crotaline venom is about 75 percent water by weight. The dried venom consists mostly of proteins and polypeptides. There are small low-molecular-weight polypeptides that cause cell damage to the linings of blood vessels, leading to massive swelling and excess fluid in the tissues (edema). Metalloproteinases destroy the infrastructure that supports blood vessels, leading to hemorrhage. Fibrinolysins break down blood clotting factors, leading to coagulopathy, the inability of the blood to clot and stop hemorrhage. Some venoms contain a component called myotoxin-a, which destroys muscle cells. Others contain the so-called Mojave toxin, which was originally isolated from the venom of the Mojave rattlesnake, but has now been found in the venoms of other rattlesnakes as well. Mojave toxin prevents nerve transmission between nerve cells and muscle cells by blocking calcium channels in the nerve and preventing neurotransmitter release, resulting in muscular weakness and respiratory arrest.

FIRST AID AND MEDICAL TREATMENT The recommendations for first aid and pre-hospital care for venomous snakebite have changed significantly over the past 25 years. Research studies of first aid treatments for rattlesnake bites are replacing dogma, and many of the "standard" treatments

Ridge-nosed rattlesnake (*Crotalus willardi*).

of the past have been abandoned because they have been shown to increase the complication rate. Unfortunately, useless or harmful pre-hospital care continues to be commonplace. Knowing what *not* to do for a snakebite victim is perhaps more important than performing any particular pre-hospital intervention.

What not to do:

NO ice!

NO heat!

NO electric shock!

NO tourniquets!

NO "pressure bandages"!

NO incision or suction!

NO Sawyer Extractor® over each puncture wound!

NO handling of dead rattlesnakes or decapitated rattlesnake heads!

What to do:

- Call for assistance and/or evacuation to the nearest medical facility for treatment and stabilization, even if no clinical signs of envenomation are apparent. Ambulance or air transport by Advanced Life Support trained and equipped personnel is preferable. The bite victim should not attempt to drive.

- If a victim is in shock, begin CPR immediately. Give intramuscular epinephrine (Epi-Pen) and antihistamines such as Benadryl® and IV fluids if available.

- Keep the victim calm and minimize physical activity.

- Try to identify the snake as long as it does not delay definitive care and does not involve additional risk of bite or injury.

- Gently immobilize a bitten extremity after removing jewelry and constrictive clothing. If a tourniquet or compression bandage has been applied previously, leave it in place.

- Begin giving intravenous saline through an unaffected extremity, if available.

- Using a pen, mark the leading edge of tissue swelling and/or bruising every 15 minutes.

- A compression band, such as an Ace wrap, may be used on an envenomated extremity if a very prolonged transport time is anticipated (many hours) or if the victim is in shock. This will likely worsen the effects of venom on the limb, but it is potentially life-saving for severe envenomations in faraway places.

Why some former treatments are no longer recommended for rattlesnake bites

Packing an envenomated extremity in ice or ice water (so-called *cryotherapy*) was popular 30 to 40 years ago and is still occasionally used by those with out-of-date medical training. Studies and experience have shown that cryotherapy is associated with increased tissue loss, including limb amputations, and increased long-term disability.

Electric shock to "neutralize" venom became popular in the 1980s after anecdotal reports from Venezuela. Multiple studies have shown that electric shock does not neutralize rattlesnake venom. In addition, complications have occurred from the electric shock itself!

Tourniquets and "pressure bandages" or "compression dressings" have been controversial treatments for rattle-snake bites for years, primarily because they do have a legit-imate role in the treatment of *elapid* envenomations, mostly outside of North America. Unlike elapid bites, rattlesnake bites cause extensive limb swelling, making pressure dress-ings and compression wraps very difficult to apply at the proper tension. Without frequent re-adjustment of the ten-sion, the continued swelling of an extremity as envenoma-tion progresses may convert the wrap into an arterial tourniquet. *If* there are systemic signs of envenomation (e.g., shock or confusion), or if there is an extremely pro-longed transport time, the use of a compression wrap or pressure bandage or even a tourniquet might be justified, with the understanding that these treatments are likely going to increase the amount of local tissue damage. In general, they should be avoided.

Incision and the use of suction devices such as the Sawyer Extractor® are also no longer recommended. The amount of venom that can be removed by immediate application of a suction device is not medically significant. Incisions, especially on the extremities, may damage underlying nerves and tendons, adding to the damage done by the venom. Mouth suction may introduce oral bacteria into the wound. Lastly, the Sawyer Extractor® appears to increase the amount of local tissue damage where it is applied. When encountered, devices such as the Extractor should be removed immediately to prevent increased tissue damage in the area under the suction cup.

Common Kingsnake or Desert Kingsnake
(*Lampropeltis getula*)
NON-VENOMOUS

Range and habitat These impressive reptiles are found all across the Southwest, particularly in mesquite-covered brushland.

Diet Kingsnakes eat lizards, birds, mammals, frogs, bird eggs, and other snakes (including rattlesnakes!).

Life span A kingsnake can live 20 years in captivity; life-span in the wild is variable.

Physical characteristics Kingsnakes vary in color from solid black to black with yellow or white bands with speck-les, and they range in size up to 3 to 5 feet (1–1.5 meters).

Behavior A non-venomous colubrid with a reputation as a powerful constrictor, the common kingsnake will even kill

and feed on rattlesnakes and appears to be immune to their venom. The desert kingsnake is actually a subspecies of the common kingsnake that is found in Texas, New Mexico, and Arizona, but not further west than south-eastern Arizona. The common kingsnake appears very nervous and agitated when first encountered, and it may put on a spectacular defensive display, rapidly vibrating its tail and attempting to appear dangerous. If captured, it is likely to defecate and release a foul-smelling musk. They are most active in early morning and evening, becoming nocturnal in the extreme heat of summer.

Reproduction Five to 17 eggs are laid in midsummer; hatching follows in late summer and early fall.

Glossy Snake (*Arizona elegans*)
NON-VENOMOUS

Range and habitat   These reptiles are concentrated in the Southwest, mostly in New Mexico, Texas, and Arizona, but also in Oklahoma, Nebraska, Colorado, and northern Mexico; they prefer areas with sandy soil and are typically associated with creosote habitats, sandy grasslands, and sagebrush plains.

Diet   Glossy snakes eat lizards, other snakes, roosting birds, and rodents.

Life span   A glossy snake can live for 10–15 years.

Physical characteristics   The glossy snake is a non-venomous colubrid that reaches lengths of about 3 to 6 feet (1–1.8 meters). The markings on the back often resemble those of many rattlesnakes, but like other colubrids, the

glossy snake has round pupils, no heat-sensing loreal pit, and no rattle. The head is also relatively small and without the triangular shape typical of rattlesnakes.

Behavior Glossy snakes are usually found in sandy or open areas. They are active at night and remain underground during the day. Large glossy snakes may bite if handled.

Reproduction Glossy snakes lay up to 24 eggs in buried clutches, and the young hatch in September and October.

Gopher Snake (*Pituophis catenifer affinis*)
NON-VENOMOUS

Range and habitat These harmless snakes are found coast-to-coast in the U.S. and throughout Mexico; their habitat includes forests, deserts, cultivated lands, and mountain ranges.

Diet Gopher snakes eat rodents, birds, lizards, and even rabbits.

Life span The gopher snake may live upwards of 20 years.

Physical characteristics The gopher snake probably generates more false-alarm calls for rattlesnakes than any other snake in the Southwest. A large snake ranging up to 9 feet in length (2.75 meters), the gopher snake has brown and tan coloration in a variable pattern that resembles that of rattlesnakes.

Behavior Active both during the day and at night, gopher snakes kill prey by constriction. When disturbed, a gopher snake will rise up to a striking position, flatten its head into a triangular shape, hiss loudly, and shake its tail; when in dried leaves or brush, they may shake their tails against debris to generate noise that resembles a rattlesnake warning. Although they are good tree climbers and will seek out active bird nests for food, they spend most of their time in burrows or on the ground.

Reproduction During the summer months, 2 to 24 eggs are laid, which hatch in the fall.

Coral Snakes (*Micrurus* and *Micruroides* species)
VENOMOUS

Range and habitat The western or Sonoran coral snake is native to central and southern Arizona, extreme southwestern New Mexico, and southward to Sinaloa in western Mexico; they are found in arid and semiarid regions in many different types of habitat including thorn scrub, desert-scrub, woodland, grassland, and farmland. They can live at elevations ranging from sea level to 5,800 feet (1,768 m) and are often seen in rocky areas, particularly in upland deserts, arroyos, and dry river bottoms.

Diet Not a lot is known about this, but they are thought to eat blind snakes, black snakes, and occasionally lizards and other small snakes; unlike rattlesnakes, which bite

and release, coral snakes and other elapids usually bite and hold onto their prey until it is subdued by the neurotoxic venom.

Life span The average life span is unknown, but it is likely many years.

Physical characteristics The Sonoran coral snake is a small, slender snake that reaches a maximum length of about 13 to 21 inches (33–53 cm). It is glossy, smooth, and brightly colored, with broad alternating bands of red, bright yellow or white, and black. The head is always black, with small beady black eyes, and the yellow or white colored

Eastern vs. Western coral snakes

In the Southwest, coral snakes are seldom seen, even by those who actively look for them. The small, weakly venomous Sonoran or Western coral snake (*Micruroides euryxanthus*) is secretive, and because of its small overall size and small fangs, it is rarely responsible for significant envenomations in humans—but that's not to say that you can't get a serious envenomation by picking one up! The Western coral snake's close relative, the dangerous Eastern coral snake (*Micrurus fulvius*), is found in the southeast U.S. but not in the Southwest. The Texas coral snake (*M. fulvius tener*) is a subspecies of the Eastern coral snake and is found in the southeastern half of Texas. It should also be considered very dangerous. South of the United States, in Mexico, Central America, and South America, there are about 30 species of coral snakes; to make thing even more confusing, all are

referred to as *coralillo* in Spanish, as are many nonvenomous snakes!

Sonoran coral snake bites are exceptionally rare, in large part because finding a coral snake is an uncommon event, and to get bitten you need to pick up or otherwise handle the snake. It therefore seems reasonable that anyone who receives a bite from a coral snake either misidentified it as a harmless mimic, or correctly identified it and probably deserves to be bitten! Fortunately, the Sonoran coral snake and its fangs are very small, limiting the amount of venom that a victim is likely to receive. Even though there are no confirmed deaths from the Sonoran coral snake, a number of people die every year from bites of the Eastern coral snake. Given the similarity of the venoms, it would seem wise to give this snake its due respect, unless you have a strong desire to make medical history.

bands are narrower than the red and black bands. All of the color bands completely encircle the body, but they are paler on the underside. The shape of the head is blunt, and as with other elapids, the small fangs are in a fixed position on the front part of the upper jaw and cannot be folded back.

Many people recognize the rhyme, "Red on yellow, kill a fellow, red on black, venom lack" as a means of identifying coral snakes. While this mnemonic works well here, it unfortunately does not work well in Mexico and further south, as coral snakes found south of the U.S. border have highly variable color banding. We also have several non-venomous snakes that have red touching yellow. In our coral snakes, the key repeating pattern is yellow, red, yellow, black. The general appearance is of a black and yellow banded snake, with red applied to the middle of the yellow bands, leaving the yellow bands smaller in size than the red or black. The Eastern and Texas coral snakes break this pattern once, making it easy to distinguish them from the Sonoran coral snake. Including the head, their first color bands are black, yellow, black—the only time that this pattern occurs.

Behavior Coral snakes spend a significant amount of time hidden underground or in rock piles, often emerging at night or late in the day during or shortly after a summer rainstorm. They may also become active during the day if the weather is overcast and cool, but they will seldom be active during the heat of the day.

When disturbed, a coral snake will often coil up and hide its head within its coiled body, then raise its tail and make popping sounds by everting the lining of the cloaca (anus) and emptying its contents. That should be enough to make everyone back off and leave! Those foolish enough to try to pin down and pick up a coral snake may find this snake to be moderately aggressive, and they can thrash, bite, and chew tenaciously. When not threatened, Sonoran coral snakes may be easily and safely observed.

Reproduction Coral snake courtship and breeding have received little study, but it is known that they usually lay two to three eggs in the summer, with the young hatching about three months later.

Effects of venom The venom of the Sonoran and other coral snakes is unlike that of rattlesnakes, but similar to that of cobras and other elapids. The venom blocks the ability of nerves to transmit signals to muscle. The end result is paralysis, as the muscles are unable to receive the necessary nerve signals telling them to contract and generate force.

During a bite, the small fangs inject venom into the skin and subcutaneous tissues, leaving tiny puncture wounds. The area around the wounds becomes somewhat tender and painful, but unlike rattlesnake bites, it does not usually swell or turn purple. The venom is then absorbed into the bloodstream, allowing it to migrate throughout the body. The first signs of serious envenomation may not occur until after a significant delay of up to six or seven hours from the time of the bite. The first symptoms may include either drowsiness or a strange anxiety, or the inability to keep the eyelids open or the eyes focused. These symptoms may be followed by nausea, vomiting, increased salivation, difficulty breathing, and death from paralysis and respiratory arrest.

FIRST AID AND MEDICAL TREATMENT The basic first aid for coral snake bites is similar to the first aid used for rattlesnake bites. The major difference is in the use of a compression bandage or loose tourniquet. Because coral snake bites do not cause swelling, it is advisable to use a compression bandage made from an Ace wrap to help prevent the spread of venom throughout the body. This bandage should be loose enough to allow one finger to easily pass under the wrap.

What to do:

- Call for assistance and/or evacuation to the nearest medical facility for treatment and stabilization, even if no clinical signs of envenomation are apparent. Ambulance or air transport by Advanced Life Support trained and equipped personnel is preferable. The bite victim should not attempt to drive.

- If a victim is in shock, begin CPR immediately. Give intramuscular epinephrine (Epi-Pen) and antihistamines like Benadryl® and IV fluids if available.

- Keep the victim calm and minimize physical activity.

- Try to identify the snake as long as it does not delay definitive care and does not involve additional risk of bite or injury.

- Gently immobilize a bitten extremity after removing jewelry and constrictive clothing. If a tourniquet or compression bandage has been applied previously, leave it in place.

- Begin giving intravenous saline through an unaffected extremity, if available.

- A compression bandage, such as an Ace wrap, should be used on an envenomated extremity if a very prolonged transport time is anticipated (many hours) or if the victim is in shock. This can be potentially life-saving for severe envenomations in faraway places.

What not to do:

NO ice!
NO heat!
NO electric shock!
NO incision or suction or Sawyer Extractor® over the
    puncture wounds!

A horse-serum-based antivenom specific for Eastern coral snake envenomations is available, but it is generally not needed for bites from the Sonoran coral snake.

Long-nosed Snake (*Rhinocheilus lecontei*)
NON-VENOMOUS

Range and habitat Long-nosed snakes inhabit the southwestern U.S. from California to Texas, and are found in prairies, brushlands, and areas of creosote desert.

Diet Their diet consists primarily of small mammals such as rodents, lizards and lizard eggs, smaller snakes, and insects.

Life span The long-nosed snake likely lives 5–15 years.

Physical characteristics The non-venomous long-nosed snake often has what appear to be bands of cream-yellow, pink or red, and black, and it is sometimes mistaken for the venomous Sonoran coral snake. The color bands are usually spotted with black or yellow, and they do not continue on the cream-colored underside of the snake.

Behavior Like many colubrids, these mild-mannered snakes are constrictors. They burrow into the sand or soil during the heat of the day, leaving only their heads exposed, and are active primarily at night.

Reproduction Long-nosed snakes frequently use abandoned burrows as nest sites. They lay anywhere from 5 to 8 eggs in midsummer, and hatchlings are born in late August or September.

Ring-necked Snake (*Diadophus punctatus regalis*)
NON-VENOMOUS

Range and habitat Although ring-necked snakes are found all over the United Snakes and Mexico, one particular species—the regal ring-necked snake—is specific to the Southwest. It prefers a moist and varied habitat and is often found at higher elevations, juniper woodlands, or desert grasslands.

Diet These snakes eat earthworms, slugs, small salamanders, lizards, and other snakes.

Life span Ring-necked snakes live about 5 to 15 years.

Physical characteristics The ring-necked snake measures about 1½ to 3 feet in length (45–90 cm) and is blue-gray to green when viewed from above, with a thin orange or red band near the neck. The underside is yellowish-orange, changing to deep red near the end of the tail.

Behavior The ring-necked snake is one of the few colubrid snakes in America that is actually mildly venomous, although not significantly so toward humans. Ring-necked snakes have rear fangs and venom glands. The temperament of this snake makes it unlikely to bite a person while being handled, and with its small fangs at the back of the mouth, it would be physically difficult for the snake to actually envenomate a person. If handled, it is likely to empty its cloaca, giving off a foul, musty substance to deter would-be aggressors.

Reproduction The ring-necked snake may breed in the spring or fall, laying clutches of up to ten eggs, which hatch in approximately eight weeks.

SUGGESTED READING

Alden, Peter, and Peter Friederici. *National Audubon Society Field Guide to the Southwestern States.* New York: Alfred A. Knopf/Chanticleer Press, 1999.

Beck, Daniel D. *Biology of Gila Monsters and Beaded Lizards.* Los Angeles and Berkeley, CA: University of California Press, 2005.

Greene, Harry W. *Snakes: The Evolution of Mystery in Nature.* Los Angeles and Berkeley, CA: University of California Press, 1997.

Hare, Trevor. *Poisonous Dwellers of the Desert: Description, Habitat, Prevention, Treatment.* Tucson, AZ: Southwest Parks and Monuments Association, 1995.

Hölldobler, Bert, and Edward O. Wilson. *Journey to the Ants: A Story of Scientific Exploration.* Cambridge, MA: Belknap Press, 1994.

Klauber, Laurence M. *Rattlesnakes: Their Habits, Life Histories, and Influence on Mankind,* second ed. Los Angeles and Berkeley, CA: University of California Press, 1997.

Mebs, Dietrich. *Venomous and Poisonous Animals: A Handbook for Biologists, Toxicologists and Toxinologists, Physicians and Pharmacists.* Boca Raton, FL: CRC Press/Medpharm Scientific Publishers, 2002.

Rubio, Manny. *Rattlesnake: Portrait of a Predator.* Washington, D.C.: Smithsonian Books, 1998.

Siegel, Richard A., Joseph T. Collins, and Susan S. Novak, eds. *Snakes: Ecology and Evolutionary Biology.* Caldwell, NJ: The Blackburn Press, 2001.

RECOMMENDED WEBSITES

http://ntrc.tamuk.edu/
(Natural Toxins Research Center, Texas A&M University)

www.embl-heidelberg.de/~uetz/LivingReptiles.html
(European Molecular Biology Laboratory Reptile Database)

http://biology.bangor.ac.uk/~bss166/update.htm
(venomous snakes systematics update)

http://spiders.ucr.edu/dermatol.html
(bites and stings of medically important venomous arthropods)

www.reptilesofaz.com/
(Arizona Partners in Amphibian and Reptile Conservation)

www.snakebitenews.com/
(snakebite antivenom news)

www.npwrc.usgs.gov/resource/distr/lepid/moths/usa/saturnii.htm
(*Hemileuca* moths)

www.rattlesnakebite.org
(a first-person account; graphic image of wound)

INDEX